WITHDRAWN

Perfidious

Man

Will Self and David Gamble

VIKING

VIKING

Published by the Penguin Group
Penguin Books Ltd, 27 Wrights Lane, London W8 5TZ, England
Penguin Putnam Inc., 375 Hudson Street, New York, New York 10014, USA
Penguin Books Australia Ltd, Ringwood, Victoria, Australia
Penguin Books Canada Ltd, 10 Alcorn Avenue, Toronto, Ontario, Canada M4V 3B2
Penguin Books India (P) Ltd, 11 Community Centre,
Panchsheel Park, New Delhi – 110 017, India
Penguin Books (NZ) Ltd, Cnr Rosedale and Airborne Roads,
Albany, Auckland, New Zealand
Penguin Books (South Africa) (Pty) Ltd, 5 Watkins Street,
Denver Ext 4, Johannesburg 2094, South Africa

Penguin Books Ltd, Registered Offices: Harmondsworth, Middlesex, England

First published by Viking 2000
1

Photographs copyright © David Gamble, 2000
Text copyright © Will Self, 2000

All photographs taken between 1979 and 2000

Set in 10/14.75pt Trade Gothic Condensed
Typeset by Rowland Phototypesetting Ltd, Bury St Edmunds, Suffolk
Printed in England by Butler & Tanner Ltd, Frome and London

A CIP catalogue record for this book is available from the British Library

ISBN 0–670–88981–4

To my father, Alfred, and to my son, Zachariah

With thanks to Lora, and to my processors/printers,
Steve at Metro and Robin Bell in Chelsea

As the last century drew to a close, I became aware of a need to express a male view on life. After twenty years of feminist literature, there seemed a distinct lack of anything truly male, so I asked Will Self if he would like to try to explain twentieth-century masculinity in a book. Each of us would comment in our own medium, allowing the viewer/reader to make their own connections, between words and pictures. As Will's words are an attempt to explain his maleness, so have I tried to explain my own maleness in my pictures, by casting my eye over the latter decade or so of the twentieth century.

My thanks to Will Self for his brilliant words and thoughts, and to all those who appear in my photos and supported my work.

David Gamble

Introduction

This is a book of photographs accompanied by a text. The photographs are about what they are about: men. Men caught in a gamut of activities and inactivities; from sleeping, to sitting, to walking, to breathing, to loving. None of them is staged, these are men caught – as it were – on the hoof. What most appealed to me about David Gamble's photographs when I first saw them was that they constituted a record of men that expressed their masculinity inadvertently. Many of the men in these photographs were manifestly not being men – they were simply being; others, of course, were working hard at it. These photographs, to my mind, caught the truth that masculinity was mostly a functional state – rather than an essence. It is possible to photograph the male body – and there are plenty of these arty cock-and-pec' shots around – but it's far harder to capture a man.

When I was a boy I never saw my father run. I don't think I can recall ever witnessing him with both of his feet off the ground, except when he was lying down. When he died, aged eighty, his face was deflated by cancer, and his cheeks were sucked in by his last, ragged gasps as he strained to reach the finish. To me, standing vigil, he looked more athletic – with his big feet akimbo, hurdling his deathbed – than he ever had before.

Not that my father was unsporting. On the contrary, at Oxford he'd been a squash and tennis half-blue. In middle age he'd been a scratch golfer. He had a wicked eye for a ball; he fixed any small globe that orbited within his reach with an almost preternatural fixity, before extending one of his long, simian arms, from his rounded shoulders, and catching it, or swiping it, or batting it away with unnerving accuracy. He seemed to reserve for tennis balls, cricket balls and golf balls a completeness of attention – of recognition even – that he denied to the small, round heads of his offspring.

But I never saw him run. When I happened along he was forty-two, at a time (the early sixties), when for a man of his class and demeanour, 'forty-two' meant elephantine flannel bag trousers, hairy tweed jackets and woollen ties. Throughout my childhood he seemed so monolithic, so leaden-based, that to imagine both his feet off the ground, or picture him with daylight streaming from under his heavy, brogue-shod size twelves, was to conceive of either a fundamental reversal of Newtonian physics, or a peculiarly Anglican instantiation of the Ascension, as a middle-aged professor of political science rose up to heaven from Hampstead Heath.

I never saw him run, and I very seldom saw him manifest any kind of alacrity at all. When he lived with us – which was continuously up until I was nine, and thereafter sporadically until I was seventeen and left myself – he wrote in a Danish Modern chair, at a kneehole desk, in my parents' bedroom. Both chair and desk creaked with the effort of absorbing the stresses imparted by his weighty ruminations on the nature of modern government, or the vagaries of regional planning policy. My mother would put lunch or supper on the table and call up to him: 'Lunch!' or 'Supper!'; and he would bellow down: 'Just coming!', then fail to appear. After five minutes she'd call up again, and receive the same reply; another five minutes would pass and she would get a third groan of imminence. It's small wonder that 'Just coming' became one of her most ambivalent catch-phrases – for she loved to hate everything he said and did.

He never ran – and he rarely hurried. He didn't run for trains or buses, he strolled in the opposite direction from crises. Far from not knowing what to do in an accident – I wonder if he rightly knew what an accident was. When the students rioted at the London School of Economics in 1968, a porter was knocked down, had a heart attack and died, on the staircase outside my father's office. He was entirely unaware of this, until phoned by my mother. Doubtless he was absorbed by the theory, while the practice was going on outside.

My father never ran, and for a man who'd never done any manual labour, he had an uncanny grasp of the fundamental principle involved in expending minimal physical effort for maximal effect. It's no wonder that golf became his game. I say 'became', but he was raised to it, and attempted to initiate my brother and me on the golf course as well. He often told us – for, as with all neurotics, bad behaviour was always justified if it had been inflicted on him already – that our grandfather had disdained even to speak to him 'until I could manage a club'. Anyway, he himself played enough golf, for sufficient years, that it was difficult to ascertain whether golf had tutored him in the exigencies of existence or, rather, he had grown to become entwined with the game, like some ambulatory, bag-toting convolvulus.

I have paradoxically fond memories of him – this round-shouldered, fat-bellied spider of a man, dominating the centre of whichever court or pitch it was he occupied, his sagging arms shooting out to loop in the ball misdirected by us, either through ire, inexperience or indifference. 'You aren't even trying!' he'd bellow, and he was right. There was very little point in trying when he was so much better than we were. It never seemed to cross his mind that a middle-aged Oxford blue with a scratch golfing handicap should by rights defeat all seven-year-old comers; it seldom occurred to him that a mere acquaintance with the rules did not, in and of itself, impart the mind of a seasoned strategist.

He taught us to play chess, backgammon, bridge and five-card stud. Then beat us at all of them. 'You don't concentrate!' he'd shout, as if it might've been possible for us to acquire a mastery of bidding conventions by thought power alone. His tactic of allowing no quarter for youth or inexperience, instead of inculcating us with the virtues of fair play and effort, on the contrary made us surly bad losers, and ultimately non-competitive. After all, what was the point of entering a competition that you couldn't possibly win? For clearly playing was not part of the game at all – it was winning the way that Dad did. In later years I found myself quite unable to explain, either to myself or to others, quite how frustrated almost any competitive situation made me feel, how tiny-dicked, how unmanned.

He had very little sense of modesty – my father. He wore bilious flannel underpants, and capacious grey flannels. This spinnaker of nether garments, together with the tails of his shirts, and even the skirt of a pullover, was cinched around his increasingly bulbous middle parts by a thin leather belt that never knew a loop in its long lifetime. With the inevitability of entropy this bundle would come undone in the course of a few holes on the links, or even a stroll through the city. Unaware and unabashed, feeling things coming adrift down below, Dad would undo his belt, unfasten his trousers, lower them slightly, rearrange the whole assemblage and then retie it. I died a thousand deaths – it drove me to drainpipes and tiny briefs.

He pissed like a horse, flattening bracken along the sides of the many paths we walked together, for ours was a father–son relationship acted out on interminable country walks. His penis was stubby and circumcised, its pink, guttering dome poking out from its ruff of black pubic hair as if it were the tonsure of some tiny monk he kept secluded in his horrible trousers. He drank many many pints of beer – then seemed to void more.

At home there were no locks on the bathroom or toilets; not that this would've made any difference, for he patrolled the house, flat-footed, incautious, and often stark naked. In the mornings he stood in my parents' room in his leprous knickers and stringy vests, varicose veins bulging at the backs of his legs like pink grapes growing on tuberous vines, and did his Canadian Airforce exercises. Having learnt these entirely from the manual, in a theoretical fashion, he performed the arm jerks and knee bends with delicious languor, as if they were an act of occidental tai chi. Even as a child I knew this was completely wrong, and I'd laugh at him and urge him to speed things up. But there was no hurrying Dad, no shrillness could affect his all-round orotundity, his decathlon of disengagement.

Of course, I realize now (and, in truth, probably understood even as a small boy), that this extreme leisureliness was a defence system, albeit one derived from his essential nature. Faced on a daily basis with the hair-trigger temper and phobic anxieties of my mother, what could a man do save retreat into the vast reserves of his own self-centred imperturbability?

The surprising thing was what a Lothario my father could be (my mother's nicknames for him were 'Pooter' and 'Polonius' – and I bet she wished that this was all there was to the man). He didn't learn to drive until he was forty, and he was a virgin until his early thirties. In the former activity he never excelled, in the latter he made up for lost time. His was a compulsively sexualized world; and it was this, mostly, that my parents recognized in each other.

At disorderly lunches on the crap terrace of our suburban semi, Dad would swill red wine. The spindly geraniums of the 1970s sprouted from between oblong, concrete slabs. His mouth, always wet and pink anyway, grew wetter and pinker. He'd select a fig from a bowl and bite into it, then display it to the rest of the table. 'Remember Birkin in *Women in Love*?' he'd pronounce, scrutinizing the roughly divided fruit, 'and what he has to say about the resemblance between a fig and a woman's –' '– Really, Peter!' my mother would break in. This happened again and again and again, throughout the aeons of my childhood.

It was not so much an open secret that theirs was an open marriage, as an open sore. An unutterably grey nimbus of lust surrounded them, permeated from time to time by the lightning strikes of anger expressed by one or the other. I grew up in this cloud of knowingness, to become that most awful of things, a jaded innocent, and a promiscuous idealist. Hampered by age, inconvenienced by the raising of small children, with which she received little or no assistance, and hobbled by avoirdupois, my mother kicked out at the dirty dog she was married to. She taught us to slow-handclap him, when, after however many 'Just comings', he finally made his entrance. She ridiculed the way he spoke, walked acted and thought. Everything about him was – she implied – fit for murder. She taught us to loathe him as she did, and in the way that she did. I grew to biological manhood with the body of a frustrated, depressed, middle-aged woman, not so much trapped – as hiding inside me.

If my father was an inadequate specimen of manhood, then there were no others on offer either. I was given leave to understand early on, that my mother's first husband had been a bastard. 'All men are bastards,' she would say, with the flat certainty of a logician proposing the first premiss of a syllogism. Naturally, given time and testosterone, I would grow to occupy this category, but in the mean time I was her 'Benjamin', her youngest, her baby-talked-to darling. Small wonder that I wanted to stay small and wondered at, like a masturbating prodigy.

So, this was the upbringing I had, from two adulterers mired in their own self-obsession, whilst all around them the sixties – that ape decade – swung through London. I grew up obsessively romantic and compulsively sexual. I grew up with absolutely no idea or conception of what it meant to be a man, or even to be masculine. My parents, with their flabby liberality, made a virtue of devolving on to us their irony and their bitterness in equal part, as if it were a particularly vile cocktail of cynicism. I drank deep. Having no positive model, my role was allocated to me on the basis of how badly I acted. This was to be manhood via the Method.

When, in puberty, I passed through my homosexual stage, I grew my hair long, read poetry, fiddled about guiltlessly. But when I began to be attracted to girls (and this flooded all same-sex attraction; it was as if a dam had burst and swept away the gay village), I became a heterosexual man standing in the wings; waiting to be manly on demand, listening for the cue to put on any act of machismo that might be construed as seductive. Without the admiring presence of a female, mine was a penile tree that fell in the forest: who was to say that it had ever existed at all? Yes, when I became a man I hung on to childish things, just as my father had kept hold of his. When we went back to Brighton, to the terraced house where he'd lived as a gentle, interwar boy, my grandmother showed us his toys, his copies of *The Magnet*, and his cricket gear, all neatly stored in his old nursery. It was as if she was waiting for the child she'd known to come back but, of course, neither of them had ever accepted that he'd left home to begin with.

My father was quite astonishingly cack-handed. In the family, the story was that he'd been unable to tie his shoes when he went away to prep school, aged seven, and that his younger brother had to tie them for him. Even as I remember it, his big fingers seemed to elude his mind's governance; and when he tied the shoelaces of golf shoes, or walking boots, it looked as if he were attempting the delicate task of mixing radioactive isotopes, using robotic arms. For my mother, the statement 'Your father can't even open a tin can' was not rhetorical. She seemed to glory in his ineptitude.

They argued — of course. They argued about anything and everything. Both of them being epigones, they always had an air of cosmic bewilderment at the idea that they were required to perform domestic tasks, but my mother attacked cooking and cleaning manfully, while my father absented himself. 'You have to have a division of labour,' he'd say, his evidently consisting in making the Danish Modern chair creak and groan, while everyone else's was all the rest.

Thirty years later, his third wife dead and buried, it was with near pity that I cleaned up the little kitchen of the house he died in. Here, in a suburb on the other side of the world, he had learnt at last to open a tin can; and the evidence of this was set out on the draining board, in the form of several of them, their sharply serrated lids raised in salute to the corpse that lay in the bedroom next door.

No, I don't blame him for anything. In as much as he failed me as a father — I failed him as a son. I was too 'wild' — as he would've put it; too immoderate; too much of a wiseacre. Too much of my mother's son. It's only this that motivates me to write about him at all: this vexed question of masculinity, of what it is to be a man. For when I come to consider it, I find I know all sorts of theories about how a man should behave — and believe me, in recompense for my own behaviours I'm keen on acquiring many more — but I find myself bedevilled when it comes to the consideration of wherein my manhood really inheres. I fondly imagine that other men, when asked this question, can reach inside themselves and feel the shape of their inner man; and that this homunculus, formed from the clay of sensibility, physicality, morality and practicality, feels them in return; that they shake hands on it, seal the masculine deal and high-five fraternity.

I've spent hardly any of my life exclusively in the company of men. I do not support a football team. What the Australians call 'mateship' has not been my estate. If I've been a man at all, it's been largely in the context of finding myself a ham alone. Whether because of my mother's espoused feminism, or her obvious misanthropy, I was helped early on to the conclusion that almost all there was to masculinity was the definition of one's sexuality in terms of aggression. Fucking and fighting, or fucking as fighting, or fighting as fucking. My own father was, according to my mother, so much less than a man; a conscientious objector in the war, who couldn't have put up a set of shelves if his life depended on it. In their relationship he supplied the fucking – she the fighting. They were a schizophrenic hermaphrodite; their marriage a screaming Procrustes, always stretched to breaking point – and beyond.

But I cannot blame them, for even as an adult, when I should by all rights have known better, I've still found myself easily taken in by negative arguments about the condition and the future of manhood. The writer J. G. Ballard once told me: 'The human male sex has become a rust bowl.' And this awesome piece of pessimism has stayed with me, oxidizing in my very masculine brain, oddly like the condition it describes.

So, when it came to the crunch, when someone asked me to write on the subject of 'masculinity', of 'manliness', of what it is to be one – I find myself seized with the most awful sense of inertia. I feel myself to be plunging towards watery extinction, weighted down with the ballast of my own masculinity, yet I cannot assay it, I do not know what it is. I feel like a kitten, spinning around and around in a vain attempt to catch sight of its own tail. Yet whenever I've voiced this sense of indeterminacy which surrounds my masculinity and inheres in my very encoding – the combinations of deoxyribonucleic acids that make me one – men smirk, women laugh, and the consensus is that I could not be any more of a man if I shaved my head, pierced my foreskin, shoved a rag soaked with butyl nitrate in my face and joined a conga line of buggery. I could not be any more of a man if I put on a khaki uniform and went on an imperialist peasant shoot. I could not be any more of a man if I modelled for a statue of Priapus.

In my late twenties I wrote a novella, *Cock*, about a woman who grew a penis and used it to rape her husband, an ineffectual alcoholic. People would ask me – and still do – what it was about. I'd give various answers: that it was about my rage with feminist arguments that all men were rapists by virtue of possessing the requisite weapon; that it was about the breakdown in gender distinctions which implied that all it was to be either one or the other was a mix and match of the requisite parts; that it was about my own nature, for, as Cocteau remarked, all true artists are hermaphrodites.

But I knew then – and know still better now – that it was about none and all of these things; that it was about my own vexed relationship with my gender; that it was about this strange situation we find ourselves in at the moment in Western societies. Marx said of the inevitable caesuras accompanying historical determinism: 'In the interregnum between two different political systems the strangest phenomena will arise.' And it's often seemed to me that we are in the interregnum between two systems of sexuality, and that the strangest phenomena are arising. Is our gender biologically or culturally determined? Are we men or hams alone? Shorn of the requirement for physical aggression or labour is there any *raison d'être* for masculinity any more?

The accepted view of sexual dimorphism is that it is one of the engines of evolutionary change; that in species where there is a radical difference between the genders you find more competition, more exclusion from breeding of the bowerbird with the duff bower, or the peacock with the lousy tail. So why do we need such a radical distinction between human genders? Are the gay clones, the effete young men, the butch lesbians, the assertive career women, all evidence of a tendency towards a third man? Or are these mere little local difficulties, wrack thrown up on the beach by the tides of cultural rather than biological evolution? Who knows – but it does feel . . . odd. It does feel as if gender proposes far more questions than it disposes; that the net result of a century or more of sexology, from Freud and Havelock Ellis to the relentless measuring and categorizing of our own era, has been an utter confusion, with gender roles flung around on the ground of the id like pick-up sticks.

It occurred to me that at least one of the reasons why my own gender status, while undoubtedly compromised, and to me indeterminate, was nonetheless indisputable to those around me, was that although it had never been reinforced by initiation, or celebrated in some corroboree, it had still always been a given. No one had ever endorsed it – but neither had they disputed it. Perhaps what I needed to do, in order to fix the position of the monument of masculinity, as it subsided into the shifting sands of change, was to seek out someone who had fought for their masculinity; who had been compelled to assert it while everyone around them was denying it. If I could talk to a person who, against all odds, had won through to proclaim themselves a man, then perhaps I'd find myself a little closer to knowing what it was to be one? Surely someone who had aspired to the condition of manhood would at least know what it was they wanted? Isn't this what's so problematic about contemporary masculinity – it doesn't seem to know what it wants – a makeover or an undoing, a retread or a retrenchment?

By the same totemic token, if I could find someone who, while branded a man, had always felt themselves to be wholly other, then possibly I could discover the sum of that masculinity which they wished to have subtracted? It occurred to me that what I required were a male-to-female transsexual and a female-to-male transsexual; that I should talk to them and discover what their perception of the issues was.

As a fisher of men I proved as prey to inertia as I was in respect of masculinity itself. I had no desire to read the background literature or wade through the plethora of writings on the subject – whether technical, confessional or political – that I knew there were. I never want to read *Orlando* again in this lifetime. Nor did I want to hang out. As a man myself I lamentably failed to hang out – why would I hang out in search of masculinity? Instead I got a friend to find me transsexuals who might be willing to talk.

The first person she came up with was a male-to-female transsexual, who had served in the forces, married and raised three children before transitioning. She now had a career that to some extent placed her in the public eye and, despite some hostile attention from the media, was managing to live her life with a high degree of acceptance in her immediate environment. I went to see her and we talked for several hours. It became clear to me very early on that she was not suitable for my purposes. She was courteous, certainly, and made honest attempts to get to grips with what I wanted to know, but she seemed uncomfortable with the degree of introspection I was asking of her. It was also plain that the last thing she felt like excavating and giving form to was a condition – namely masculinity – that she'd wanted rid of more than anything else.

It struck me, in conversation with this attractive, pleasantly spoken woman who was once a man, that perhaps her reticence was a function of her transsexual status itself? That maybe her haziness of recall about her relationship with her gender before she transitioned was a function of her sense of ill-fitting within that gender category? Maybe all transsexuals were incapable of insight in this regard; and further, believing as they now mostly do, that their status at birth is one of having been born into the wrong body, my questions about having to struggle to attain the gender they desired were beside the point. This woman had been in no doubt that she was a woman – it was the world that was confused, the world that labelled her 'man'. It followed from this that to ask her about what it had been like to be a man was equally unproductive; for her it had been a performance, pure and simple. To ask for profundity from her on the subject was akin to expecting an actor playing Hamlet to come up with vital insights on the origins of existentialism.

The thing I found saddest, and in a way most bathetic, about this woman, was that she was worried about any possible publicity arising from her participation in this project, not because she feared the reaction of friends, family or colleagues (they all knew and accepted or rejected her already), but because she evidently still hoped to enter new relationships in which she would be able to pass as a woman, and there would be no immediate doubts in the other's mind about her gender.

That my interlocutors were prepared for their words to be made public was not an essential part of the deal for me. I was happy to disguise them in any way they felt appropriate, but this woman's need to believe that she would 'pass' in this fashion – something that I believed unlikely – alerted me at the deepest level to her vulnerability. Even if I wasn't going to involve her in further publicizing of her transsexual status, the intense self-scrutiny my questioning would call forth might well make it impossible for her to sustain herself in this optimistic view of her future. I decided to leave her be.

The next person my friend lined up for me to see was Stephen Whittle, a lecturer in law at Manchester University, a leading light in Press for Change, the transsexual pressure group, and familiar to me through the other kind of press. Stephen Whittle was the transsexual man who had tried to have his status as the parent of the four children he's brought up, together with his partner Sarah Rutherford, recognized in the European Court of Human Rights. According to British Law, while Sarah – who conceived the children through AI (Artificial Insemination) – is indisputably their mother, Stephen, whom she has been in a steady relationship with for over twenty years, and who has acted in every respect apart from biologically as the children's father, had no rights at all. If one of the children had an accident at school the staff had no legal requirement to inform him.

I knew that Stephen Whittle's case had proved unsuccessful, but beyond this and the bare facts about him published on the Press for Change website, I knew nothing else. My friend ascertained that he was prepared to speak to me; I then called him and arranged to visit him at his house, in a suburb of Stockport, south of Manchester. I told him very little about the project, except that I was conducting a series of interviews with transsexual people for a text that was to accompany a book of photographs of men. I wanted to weight the success or failure of the endeavour entirely on the encounter. As with my first subject, I felt it was essential that whatever transpired between me and Stephen was not freighted with expectation; I also think that I realized at an intuitive level that one of the things that transsexual people must find hardest to deal with is the atmosphere of prurience which surrounds any enquiry launched by non-trans people into their lives.

After we had met and talked several times, and Stephen had spoken about his life with candour and insight, he told me that this was indeed the case; or rather, he told me that he had never met a heterosexual man who did not at some level maintain a prurient mien (whether covert or overt) when talking to him. Put bluntly: heterosexual men simply could not get over the issue of what kind of genitals Stephen had and what sexual use he put them to.

I won't make the claim that I'm devoid of such prurience, or that I'm incapable of framing these kind of questions but, for me, when it came to developing a relationship with Stephen, these issues were as circumscribed by good manners and the gradual attainment of intimacy as they would be with any other man. As I've said: I have not spent a great deal of my life with other men; and certainly, the kind of men I have spent my time with have not been in the habit of either asking, or telling each other, what their genitals are like, or what they do with them. I could see no reason not to extend this common courtesy to Stephen.

Beyond this, perhaps unlike other men, I had no preconceptions about whether or not Stephen was what he claimed to be – namely, a man. My whole manner of enquiry into the subject, my own habits of mind – both as a man and as a writer – inclined me to accept whatever he would say at face value. I was not looking for him to convince me of his gender identity at either a dialectical or a physical level; I wanted to enquire into the nature of masculinity with him (he was, after all, an academic specializing in the legal theory surrounding trans-gender issues), and let our conversations illuminate our feelings and thoughts about masculinity, whether they be shared or at variance.

Of course, it would be entirely disingenuous to claim that I was not influenced by everything about Stephen Whittle: his home, his family, his appearance, the way he spoke, the way he held himself. But I was open to all of these impressions as fully and as non-prejudicially as possible. It wasn't that I was looking for him to prove himself as a man to me – and thereby illuminate what it was that was inherently 'masculine' about being one – but what I did want was for every aspect of who he was to be allowed to speak for itself.

Suffice to say, within the first hour of talking to Stephen I realized that I was in the presence of an exceptional individual, whose life experience and capacity to enquire into it could not help but illuminate the very questions I was seeking answers for. And by the end of the second time we met, I abandoned any thoughts of speaking with anyone else and decided to dedicate this project to Stephen. Stephen told me early on that he had not talked to anyone besides me about his life, in this depth and to this extent (saving, of course, for Sarah and his close friends within the trans community who had accompanied him through it). He also told me that he felt able to open up to me in a deep way. He had always intended to tell the story of his life, but was uncertain about how it should be done. Sensationalism of any kind was to be avoided at all costs. In a sense, my arrival provided him, by chance, with the opportunity he sought.

For my part, as a writer, I understood early on that Stephen and I had between us the kind of rapport that, if tended carefully, might produce a unique kind of testament. As I say, I had no preconceptions about how to deal with the material imparted by Stephen during our conversations, but one point was clear to me from the outset: it was important that he have the right to veto the appearance in print of anything at all. This would be nothing if it was not an exercise in trust.

We met and talked four times over a period of some five months. Three of these occasions were at his home in Stockport, and one was at mine in London. The conversations lasted between one and three hours. Full transcripts were made, and I then edited them so as to eliminate my questions and observations. Stephen then read the edited transcripts and made a few, very minor, alterations, either to elucidate points he felt were unclear, or to protect friends and family. I stress – these were very minor alterations.

It matters, therefore, how you approach this text. If you read it looking for prurient answers to prurient questions – you will not find them. If you skip through it hoping to chance upon the answers to the questions about masculinity that I have proposed – then you will be disappointed. Rather, this text should be viewed as a whole and, like Stephen, allowed to speak for itself. The answers to many of the questions you might wish to propose about masculinity, about the impact of feminism upon it, and about being transsexual, are all here – but they are filtered through the reticulation of an unusual life story. If I was instrumental in prompting this level of enquiry, then I have done a good job, but that is all I have done; the insights themselves are Stephen's alone, just as the life is his alone.

At Stephen's home we talked, sitting on a divan, in his partner Sarah's room. It's a comfortable study-cum-workspace, neatly furnished with a desk, a computer and a dressmaker's form. This headless, genderless torso was an apt totem, given the nature of our discussions. When Stephen and Sarah first met, in the early seventies, Stephen was already passing as a man, and taking hormones, but he was yet to undergo any surgery. One of the things Sarah Rutherford has said about being Stephen's partner is that, perforce, it completely alters people's perceptions of her as a woman: the same prurient searchlight that gets trained on Stephen then wavers across to fix her in its beam. I have no wish to contribute to this, and while I believe that it's important for the reader to have some sense of the family Stephen and Sarah have founded together, I want to make it clear that this is Stephen's story – not Sarah's; and that while Sarah has read and approved this text, her own life and opinions remain to be recorded in another place.

Nevertheless, my impression of Sarah was that she was a woman who was in a long-term relationship with a man. If you want to call this kind of woman 'heterosexual' – then do by all means. If you want to take my word for it that Sarah Rutherford is a very attractive, forthright, intelligent, capable woman, who seemed to be not in one iota strange or peculiar – then please do.

We talked in her room, and very occasionally Sarah would come in to recount some essential aspect of her and the children's day. At the end of each of the Stockport sessions we had supper together: Stephen; Sarah; their long-time friends and housemates Alex and John; the au pair and myself. The younger children were sometimes in bed by then, but their oldest daughter, Eleanor, often came into the conservatory area where we ate and stopped for a while to chat. The conversation between the adults was wide-ranging and by no means fixated upon issues of gender and sexuality, despite the fact that between us six adults there were almost as many different gender statuses and sexual orientations. After all, when six people from different races meet together, they don't necessarily talk about racism or miscegenation. The food was excellent.

Tolstoy said that: 'All happy families are the same, but every unhappy family is unhappy in its own way.' I don't wish to make a facile statement – but the Whittle/Rutherford family is manifestly a happy one. What this means is, that even if I wanted to, I'd find it hard to write about them with any degree of objectivity. Alex and John have lived with Stephen and Sarah for many years and are fully accepted as family members, but the impression I received (and it was one which Stephen to some extent reinforced), was that he and Sarah were, respectively, patriarch and matriarch. All the adults share duties and responsibilities within the home, and all of them are involved to a greater or lesser degree with the child-rearing. It's a comfortable, rambling, detached, turn-of-the-last-century house in a leafy suburb. The kind of house that has a tiled hall, herringbone parquet floors and mullioned windows. The furniture and decoration is unostentatious – but good. This is a home full of books and paintings and music. This was a home, I sensed, where disputes are resolved and tensions dissipated. This was a home, I grasped, where there resided a firm consensus on ethics; where the adults agreed on what was to be done. This was a home very unlike the one I grew up in – this was a home where the men and the women knew what their respective roles were, and found them comfortable. This was a home where no one bleated on about the division of labour as an excuse for not doing any.

I don't wish to idealize this – after all, I was only a guest – but you get a nose for these things, especially if your own upbringing consisted in having it repeatedly broken. In their home I felt that peculiar nostalgia for a state which I had myself never really experienced – a dangerous kind of sentimentality. And as for Stephen, how did I regard him? Completely and incontrovertibly as a man – of that I had no doubt. An unusual man certainly – but no more unusual than I am myself. Wherein does his masculinity consist? In all of him: in his appearance, his demeanour, his manner of expressing himself – in his very quiddity; his quality of this-is-Stephenness. But still more importantly – and this is why I've written about the family at all – his manhood resides in his relationships with it, as a partner, as a father, as a patriarch. These aspects of Stephen's masculinity are far more important to me than whether he's big or small, bearded or clean shaven, let alone what kind of genitals he has.

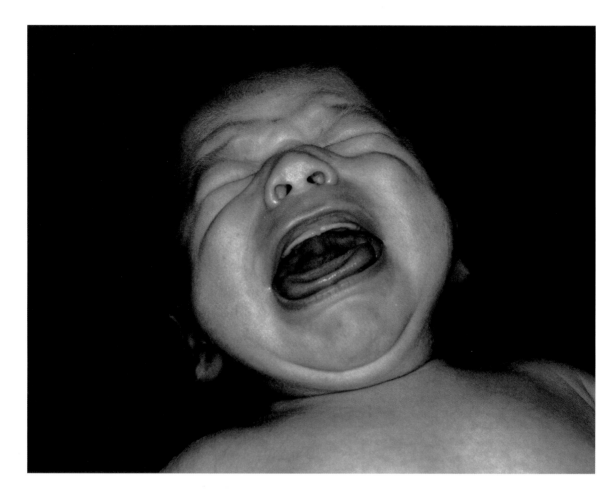

Stephen Whittle

If somebody asked me for an easy answer I would say I was born a boy – it was just that nobody could see it. And then when I grew up and I was big enough and old enough, I did something about it to make sure people *could* see it. But that is actually a sort of easy, off-the-cuff answer. It is obviously much more complex than that. And certainly I can remember, at eighteen or nineteen, seeing the shrinks and them sort of asking the obvious question, um, well, the question was 'Do you feel like a man or do you feel like a woman?' And, hold on a minute! Let's get into the complexities of that, the reality is, I knew that biologically I was female, I had had an immense amount of input as a child that was meant to say that I was going to grow up as a teenage girl, a woman in some shape or form. But all that made me feel incredibly uncomfortable. It wasn't until I was quite old that I was able to pin down what was uncomfortable about it. And, you know, I couldn't say that I wanted to live as a man till I was probably about seventeen or so. And for a long time I tried to pin down for myself whether in fact what I was was a transvestite woman . . . and the easy answer perhaps was to say, 'Perhaps I'm a lesbian, perhaps I'm a dyke,' but actually that didn't fit in with my sexuality and my sexual orientation at all. It was much more complex than that. So trying to pin down in some way what, actually, at what point do you know you should live as a man, is actually a very, very heavy, multilayered question. This is why for a lot of people, when they're thinking about transition from one gender to another, they take an awful lot of time thinking about it. Because you're very aware that in fact you have a positioning which sort of shifts just slightly on one side of the scale. In other words, that in fact you're not a feminine woman, in my case, but you're not actually a man at that point, you're just this side of the scale, y'know, you're perceived as a masculine woman, you're perceived as a butch dyke, you're perceived as someone who's a bit weird and doesn't conform. And then you sort of step over that line, through the aid of hormone treatment, some surgery or whatever . . . but you don't quite make it into full manhood, ever. Because you're also incredibly aware that you have none of that background. When I theorize I talk about some essence of the essential self, and people understand. But when you cross over that line you don't ever gain full entry into a man's world.

I was brought up in Manchester on the Wythenshaw Estate; there were five of us. I had two older sisters and two younger brothers, and my first brother was born when I was two. And so, as I was growing into my gender awareness I was aware that there was a model preceding and a model coming afterwards. Um . . . it was very much that the household was quite Victorian in its concepts and, you know, it's actually quite hard to explain to people, but I didn't realize there was a physical difference in bodies between boys and girls until school-playground jokes started – I was about nine or ten. Because I'd never seen my two brothers naked and never seen my father naked. And the concept of seeing a naked body was not there. So, as far as I was concerned, from being quite young, everybody's bodies were just the same. Never conceived of different bodies at all. And then I can remember being four or so, when my brother was about two, and I had another brother who'd been born, and they were bought – given – matching suits, which consisted of little fawn trousers and a jacket with a velvet collar. And it really, sort of, hit me quite hard at that age, that I really, really, really wanted those clothes but I wasn't going to be allowed to have them. And that that sensation, of clothing being a differentiation, was quite a powerful thing. There were things that I was meant to wear that I just couldn't understand why anybody would want to wear – they were hideous, they were ugly, they were made of appalling material, they felt terrible, the actual sensation of this clothing was dreadful; and my mother says she can remember when I was about five, and we'd had a huge row about me going to school with this skirt on. I hadn't gone to school for about three days, I'd screamed blue murder over it, and she'd bribed me by making me a pair of trousers to wear in the evenings, and this meant I never got out of them. I couldn't ever change and that was it!

My father was originally a cleaner at a petrochemical company, but he ultimately became plant manager after an accident. He got a desk job after learning to read and write at home because he couldn't read or write or before that. When we were young he learned to read and write, went to college. He was a guy who'd left school at the age of nine, become a cobbler, gone into the Army at the age of fourteen, done the D-Day landings at the age of sixteen. He'd also been in the Army jail for a couple of years. My relationship with him as a child was always quite distant.

From when I was very young I intensely disliked his view on life. I remember him discovering from a neighbour that the guy who lived out back – who was black – had a job. Then he was really, really angry that a black man should have a job, because he was still at this point just a cleaner. I must have been just six, but I was absolutely horrified – even at that age – that he could judge someone by the colour of their skin. So we had an intrinsic dislike of each other right from the beginning, the things he thought were important issues in life were just not what I thought at all. I couldn't understand how he could be racist, I couldn't understand why books were not really allowed in the house unless they were science books. If you did something he considered wrong he beat you first, and your explanation was not even considered, it wasn't an issue. So most of my childhood was spent in some sort of fear of him. Y'know, we spent a lot of time very frightened of the guy. He never beat you to the point where you were black and blue or anything like that, but you certainly felt a constant fear. And right until leaving home there was an incredible fear of this guy. I can remember my sisters and I standing on different street corners waiting for him to go to bed. He'd come in from the pub about half ten, eleven, and he'd sit and watch telly till three a.m., and we'd all stand on the street waiting for him to go to bed. Because if you went in the house in that space between him actually arriving home and him going to bed you'd be in deep shit. You just had to make sure he didn't see you.

I justify it now by the fact that he must've been intensely jealous of anybody else getting anything that he thought came on a plate. Y'know, I remember being walloped in front of the rest of the kids when I passed my O levels . . . he lined them up, you know, and he'd give you a good thrashing, for various reasons. Well, when my sister said she was going to get married he did that – she was eighteen. And he did that when I passed my O Levels – just so's I knew I was no better than anyone else. I remember him once whopping my mother for wearing trousers on a camping holiday.

My mother was somebody who obviously provided some level of protection for us, but at the same time she was always tired, she was working full time as well. She had to have a job, that was the rule, she had to have a job as well, y'know sort of thing. And certainly, from my being about eleven, she was planning her escape, you know, she was actually saving up bits of money all the time. So you felt like, um, she was someone you could approach so long as he wasn't around. And if it was anything which she would have to refer to him, well, you didn't, you know. So it was quite a distant relationship. She knew no other way, and what she was doing was, she was waiting till most of us could leave home, and that was exactly what she did. She waited until I was eighteen, and my youngest brother was going into the Merchant Navy, that meant she was left with one of my brothers at home for another year . . . and at the end of the year she moved him out, sold the house and moved on . . . I think she found the whole thing incredibly hard.

My brothers and sisters were really quite close, and we still have a closeness that comes of actually having had these experiences . . . the plotting to get rid of the badminton racket which he used to belt us with, at one point, and we plotted to throw it into a dustbin. It's so hard when you're brought up in a very working-class culture where these things seem to happen to most people anyway, or rather you don't find out that it doesn't happen to other people, you just presume it's the norm.

I was the middle child, and I was very much the different one. My two sisters went round in a pack, and my two brothers went round in a pack, and I sort of sat in the middle. When we were very young – up to being about six or seven – I was allowed to play with my brothers in whatever games they were playing, but then it sort of got stopped, and I can remember moving house when I was about eight, getting into the most horrendous trouble for playing with my brothers out in the street. I could certainly play their games when they were not definitely boys' games. But as soon as the games shifted, as soon as they reached six or so, and shifted into boys' games, that was when the hatchet came down on that.

We moved to an area of Manchester where everybody played in the street. There were specific gangs that went round, and there was the older girls' gang, and it was definitely an older girls' gang – there wasn't an older boys' gang going around at the time – and there was a younger boys' gang. I remember on two or three occasions trying to break into the girls' gang, and getting, y'know, real strong rejection about wanting to be part of them . . . I can remember being absolutely beaten up by a couple of them once, with everyone standing around screaming and shouting . . . everybody, y'know, they didn't want me, and I didn't fit and I didn't belong.

This was when I was about eight, and I was intensely unhappy, very much wanting to participate in the boys' world and the boys' games and everything else that went on there, and just not being allowed to, and trying to fit into this slot of the girls and just not being wanted. And y'know, feeling totally isolated at that point.

And it was bound up with clothing, it was bound up with what you got for Christmas, it was bound up with the way your hair was cut. There was no sort of sensation of sexuality. And on the whole I would think sexuality and sexual orientation is something that actually comes quite late for a lot of people, particularly if they're male to female. Female to male transsexuals probably have an earlier awareness of sexuality and sexual orientation. But it comes post puberty, it comes with the realization that you do have a sexual body, prior to that it's sort of thrown away, it's not on any agenda. When puberty does hit, the intense hatred of your body is just so profound as your body starts to change, it's absolutely the most immense thing. The first thing that happened to me in terms of puberty was menstruation . . . It was like God's punishment – it happened in church! And I had no idea what it was, I must have been around eleven, and I'd never heard of periods, I mean, there had been jokes in the school playground which I just did not understand, I had no idea what they meant . . . to discover you're bleeding in church was just the most horrendous thing. I mean, I didn't know whether I was dying or what. And I mentioned it to someone in the church, and they sent me home, where my mother whisked me upstairs and cleaned me up and gave me some sanitary towels, said I had to wear these – that's what you wear. She gave me very minimal explanation. About a year later she left a book by my bedside to read. As for my older sisters, they never discussed it at all. Never. I think if I'd been one of them – this sounds a really strange statement – but if I'd been a girl like them I may have been able to cope with it better, because I think they talked between themselves.

The people I wanted to be close to were the people I fell in love with. From quite an early age – twelve – I can remember having crushes. First of all on the gym teacher, then a sixth-former, and by the time I reached seventeen the crushes were on people in my own class, and I thought, Shit! You're meant to grow out of this . . . I also had girls who had crushes on me, going down the school, as I got older. So it was accepted that that was what you did. You didn't talk about it a great deal but it was known that everybody had a crush on somebody, y'know, at some point. It's just that mine went on and on!

Throughout that time, I felt my life was a total and utter performance, and I always felt that, I did throughout my whole life – certainly from puberty onwards – in terms of what was expected, in terms of what I could get away with, in terms of appearing to be almost normal, but at the same time trying to keep a little bit of me there. So, for example, the school uniform changed so you could get away without wearing a tie, but I wore a tie all the way through. The Guide uniform changed, too . . . and I stuck with the traditional one. So I kept a little bit of me always.

The way I was thinking as my ten-year-old self was that I could not for the life of me imagine growing up to be a teenage girl and then a woman. I looked at my older sisters, I looked at my mother, I looked at women in the family, and I thought, I cannot become one of them. But it wasn't that I wanted . . . I knew that I ought to be a boy . . . sort of different from, y'know . . . 'I am a boy.'

When I was ten, we had a sports day at school, and I was meant to go in the girls' races, and I had the sensation of — and it really was such a strong realization — of being sent to go in the wrong race, and I was always going to be in the wrong race, that was awful. I remember, then, at ten, just not knowing how I was ever going to live the rest of my life. That was why I was desperate to get into the adult section of the library. I wanted to find a solution. From eleven I got permission and would sit in the medicine and psychology section, frantically reading everything I could — I could perform an appendectomy if needs be! I read anything that might have any bearing, ultimately . . . and certainly, when I was fourteen or fifteen I did debate . . . well . . . could you remove your breasts yourself?

But I never saw masculinity — say, in my father's model — as being the slightest bit attractive. So, throughout that period of trying to gauge how not to grow up to be a woman — and an old woman in particular — I couldn't grasp the idea of growing up to be someone like my father. So I spent a lot of time looking for other masculine models. I had a French teacher in primary school, he was kind, he taught you, he listened to you, he had a beard . . . as well as all sorts of other things. I mean, secondary characteristics of masculinity were so desirable, they were overwhelmingly desirable, but I still couldn't think in terms of a penis, it was all about how you physically looked . . . and it was attractive in every shape, it was attractive as something I wanted for myself, it was attractive in other people, and this provided me with all sorts of real issues about sexuality and where my sexual orientation was. I hadn't the faintest idea. I'd read the books and I'd think, Um, well, I'm meant to be a lesbian if I'm like this, 'cos I also knew I found women very attractive, and there was no idea that you could have any other sexuality apart from being straight, as a woman, or a lesbian as a woman. And the idea that you could actually change sex was not feasible at all. I spent so much time reading books and thinking,

Somebody must have been born a girl and grown up to be a man. It must happen to somebody!

It felt like a physical illness. It didn't feel like a mental state, it felt like a physical thing, so overwhelmingly physical that there had to be some biological cause for it, there had to be something, there had to be something wrong with my chromosomes, kind of thing. I felt that I was trapped in childhood, I was trapped but I didn't want to go forward, but that also felt like a trap, because, y'know, whether I liked it or not I was going to go forward . . . and . . . in fact I had, three or four times as a teenager – probably starting at about fourteen, when I, y'know – tried to top myself.

It was total anguish. But also absolute desire to stop it, to stop it going any further. And to say, 'Let's draw a line. *Here*. The first bit was tolerable, this bit's becoming horrendous, the future is appalling, let's just stop it here.' And . . . and trying to stop it there. Y'know, sit and think, well, how many aspirin do you actually have to take? And, y'know, you'd take as many as you could and then you'd throw up for the night . . . and then you'd think, well, that obviously wasn't enough.

My feeling is that the whole concept of gender dysphoria, the very wide concept, is a really common reason for many adolescents trying to, and actually succeeding in killing themselves. That, along with bullying . . . the whole notion of being an outsider. To not be an outsider any longer – to just not be any longer. And the more I talk and listen to trans people, and listen to students – y'know, my door's the door they knock on, with their assorted problems, their pregnancies, their arranged marriages – you realize it's this notion of feeling outside of your culture, outside of your society, that you're never, ever, going to fit in. You just think, Let's just stop it, at this point. Y'know – end it, now.

What made it possible for me to survive was firstly – and most profoundly – the school that I went to. I went to an all-girls school near Manchester that was a direct-grant school. I got a scholarship to it. It was a school with no punishment and no praise, that was the whole principle of it, and they did indeed follow that line. Nobody was ever singled out as being better than anybody else, and nobody got punished. It was a group ethos. Eccentricities were totally accepted, they were seen as being strange, but at the same time they were not a reason for a telling-off. There was no reason whatsoever for them to make me conform as long as I stayed within the bounds of the uniform rules and behaved in a reasonably presentable way. I have to say it was the school that made me the man I am today!

My mother actually insisted to my father that I was going to take the entrance exam to the school, and I had been dreading the idea of going to the same school as my sisters. And I think that was one of the occasions my mother did realize she had to draw a line. I think she was aware that I was very different.

I started cross-dressing at fifteen or sixteen. I started going into the wardrobes of my brothers and borrowing their jackets and sneaking out. I'd actually go out in public, yes, and try and pass myself off as, y'know, a lad. It worked better than it ever did passing myself off as a girl! Just going into a shop – but these were rare occasions, because the opportunities didn't come up very often. But I'd go to town on a Saturday afternoon, having pinched a jacket off my brothers, and I'd put on my school shirt and tie, put on the jacket and go to the shops, go round the shops as a lad. I don't think anybody saw me. But they were rare occasions, as I say, I spent most of my time being busy so that I could avoid thinking about it, and it was almost like an overwhelming thing that happened every now and again. The other thing that happened was that when it actually came to . . . sort of . . . masturbation, I would have to do that in some way, shape or form, cross-dressed.

Looking back, there was never an ambiguity about my orientation. I think all the time I fancied both men and women. Y'know, there were no ifs and buts about it, there was a certain sort of man I found really desirable and a certain sort of woman I found really desirable. But the desire I had was strongly rooted in perceiving myself as being a man. The fantasy of masturbation always involved me being a man, always. But the person who I fantasized about could be a certain sort of man or a certain sort of woman.

I was a male bisexual trapped inside a female body! My sexual orientation – bisexual – I always found a really difficult one, because it doesn't fit really with someone who's a trans person to say you're bisexual, because, y'know, how the hell can you – if you're trans – think of people in clear sexual groupings!

At that point in my life gender was two quite distinct things, depending on whether you were a man or a woman. If you were a woman you were an object of somebody else's desire, always. You were always destined to be subservient, not have any seniority. It wasn't exactly that there were no strong female role models, it's just that I thought you'd never, ever, ever be able to dictate the rules, never be in total charge, never, ever be able to take charge of your own home, your own bedroom particularly, and how you presented yourself. You'd always, always have to walk ten paces behind. What that felt like was . . . y'know . . . if I was going to grow up to be a woman, it meant I would always have to do what somebody else told me to do, whether it was domestically, workplace, sexually, whatever. I would never have complete choice for myself unless I became a spinster. But to be a spinster still meant I was going to grow up into this horrendous, horrible body.

At that age I had very much decided in my mind that I would never have children but that it was an immense loss, that the only way I could ever survive was if I chose never to have children, in fact if I chose never to have a relationship, if I chose to be the schoolteacher spinster. That was the only way I could ever envisage myself, as a schoolmarm spinster who hid her body between clothes that were as masculine as they could be, and that I just wouldn't look at myself.

Then I read an article in a women's magazine, it had a picture of somebody, a guy, walking through a gate. It was a shadowy picture of someone with a donkey jacket on, and it was a story about a female to male transsexual. I just went, 'That's it! It's possible. I'm gonna do it!' Right. How am I gonna do it. How? Right, first I've got to get out of school, but I've got to be independent, I've got to be somebody who can work, I've got to have ways of making money. That means I've got to pass my exams, I've got to leave home as quickly as possible, I've got to try and find work, y'know, and I've got to find the doctor. It was, like, headlong. I was seventeen, it was just before Christmas in my lower-sixth year. From then on it was just a headlong race to try and get there. I gave myself four years. Twenty-one, right, I'm gonna have this by the time I'm twenty-one and if I haven't got it, that's it! Then I'll go back and kill myself. And by the time I'm twenty-one, with a bit of luck, I'll know how to do *that* properly.

Because every night I went to bed I'd think about how I could kill myself. As I got up to being seventeen, these thoughts were just continuous. I thought about it every weekend, and probably once a year I tried it really seriously, once a month I tried it semi-seriously, y'know . . . I was too much of a coward to slit my throat! But I used to take pills . . . and, y'know, I have to think . . . well, I've got IBS (Irritable Bowel Syndrome) now, and it's almost certainly because I took so many aspirin, so the whole thing was pervading my life all the time. Ninety-nine percent of my time I just performed, performed, performed, really well for everybody else – except the little bit I kept: the eccentricity. Then, about once every blue moon, I'd just get so angry that I'd try and throttle somebody.

I nearly put one girl in hospital. They had to call the ambulance! She told me to piss off, and I just couldn't take anybody telling me to piss off, I was too busy telling myself to piss off, thank you. Throttled her, y'know. Raging. When I lost it, I just raged. I felt that I'd dropped into a huge black hole filled with the most horrendous sort of thick shit. My body disappeared completely, I became this empty, huge bag of shit. I smelt bad, I felt bad, and I had no awareness in those moments that I was doing anything to anybody. It wasn't until I stopped doing it – or was stopped – that, I mean . . . I can't to this day remember having my hands round anybody's neck.

I had sexual contact in my teens, but it was only ever with boys and it couldn't be said to be girlfriend/boyfriend, because it was never of choice. It was a case of, 'Oh fuck, we're in the bus shelter this is what you're supposed to do.' You'd go out to a pub with a disco in it where people would cop off with the boys. I was blonde and slim – it made for a bit of a pain at the time really. And I've long concluded that most men prefer sporty-looking women anyway . . . who look as if they're good to get on with it, not going to be doing their nails all the time. And some guy would be very nice, and I'd think, Oh, all right, I'll have a dance with him. And he'd say, 'Can I walk you home?' and you'd get to the bus shelter or wherever else it was, and you'd think, Oh fuck, we've gotta go through this . . . um, can we do something to make sure I don't get pregnant, 'cos I really can't deal with that one? Well, y'know . . . I could understand that they wanted to have sex.

If I did get pregnant, everything I'd thought about, I'd debated was possible in my life, would end. I certainly couldn't imagine being able to have a sex change if I had a baby. I'd had a horrendous experience which was almost rape with a friend of my father's who'd met me in town . . . um, when I was dressed as a lad, by chance. And he'd seemed sort of OK about it and said he'd give me a lift home. He said, 'I tell you what, we'll go for a drive first.' So we went out on to the hills, and he said he knew what would cure me. Then he dropped me off at home. I couldn't ever tell anyone about it and was fucking terrified that I'd get pregnant.

I'd always had a male persona. He was called Peter from the time I was ten. Y'know, that was who I really was. Um . . . he was gay, and he had a whole series of adventures going on in my head all the time. Every now and again he'd be real – I'd be him. He had his own story and his own life and his own place to live. Until I was about fourteen or fifteen I used to go to sleep every night by telling myself the next bit of the story, and he'd have all sorts of adventures. It was something I lived in and survived in, an absolutely essential part of me. But I knew that Peter wasn't true, I knew this was a story, it was a dream, it was a waking dream. I day-dreamed him all the time, and if I got a moment's peace and quiet I'd day-dream him. Peter was the name I first changed to when I transitioned, and then everybody else said it was too old-fashioned. Stephen was chosen by other people . . . But actually I often think I'm still Peter in my head; there's a definite part of me that's still that guy.

After leaving school, Stephen went to teacher-training college, where he continued to investigate the nature of his sexual orientation. While convinced that he wanted a sex change, at that time – in the early seventies – it still seemed an impossibility.

I managed to get a room in a small house which was shared with five girls, . . . um, one of whom was blatantly and obviously a lesbian; in fact, two of them were, but different lesbians totally, one was very butch and one was femme. The one who was butch had a motorbike and I thought, Well, perhaps I can be like her? The one who was femme, I thought, Well, perhaps I can sleep with her and see what it's like? And that was the first woman I slept with, and it was just appalling, it was dreadful. I felt like I wanted to throw up, it was absolutely nauseating, I couldn't stand the smell of her body, I couldn't stand the feel of her body, I couldn't stand the fact that she wanted to feel my body. There was nothing in the slightest bit pleasurable about it. I actually had to bail out, I had to say, 'Listen, I can't do this, I cannot do this.' And I went and hung over the bathroom sink, like I wanted to gag, y'know, and I was thinking, Well, that's that. At the time I had also met a guy who was a local policeman, at the climbing club, and thought, Well, y'know, um, he was OK . . . Actually, at this date I had so many of them it was just unbelievable, there was him, there was Adam, there was John . . . y'know . . . I was being actively pursued by these guys, and, um, I liked all of them. They didn't mind that I wore trousers all the time, and I told every single one of them what I was intending to do. Not one of them minded, I don't know if they thought it was ever really going to happen. But I think they actually liked me, and they were good men, we were great mates. We got on really well and I slept with all of them, once or twice, three times, not often, 'cos I was only there three months. It was good mates having sex together, it was very much good mates having sex together. And the sex was much more enjoyable, I mean, not brilliant – not as I would now know sex. When you're eighteen or nineteen – what's good sex! It's all pretty awful . . . it's all a bit intense in terms of trying to get off, and it's all about coming. But it happens and it's not awful and I didn't feel terrible about it. But I never took off my clothes, only the bare minimum. I never felt there was never anything nice about my body, there was never any sort of, Oh, you've got a really nice body. Y'know, we weren't interested in the body, full stop.

Then December came and we had to do our first teaching practice, and we had this big lecture on what we should wear, which was, basically, we had to wear, as women, dresses. So I got out this shirtwaister dress my mother had bought me that I'd worn on two previous occasions, I got this out, went to the shops, and I bought a pair of tights. And I went off, and before I even went I knew it was a fucking disaster. Eleven o'clock in the morning I thought I was going to go mad, I really, really thought I was going to go mad, I thought I was going to run around the place screaming. I got through to the end of the day, and I thought, I just can't, I just can't, I'm not gonna do it. So I went on the sick, and I thought, I've just got to get out of this, I can't ever go back and do that again. I can't pretend anything apart from — y'know, I can try and perform this woman I'm meant to be — but I can't just pretend it any longer. It's much more intense than that. So anyway I left teacher-training college at the end of December.

I managed to get this job with accommodation at a Girl Guide Association conference centre, so I went straight there from teacher-training college in the December and thought, Right, now I'm here. It was really interesting when I went there, because there was this woman who used to come and do odd jobs . . . and she was a man. It was obvious. Not that she was a male to female transsexual — she was born female, but, my god, she was a man. It was, no question about it that this person I was talking to was a man. This person who I saw in front of me was a man. Dressed in jeans and a jumper, with short hair, but wasn't a lesbian. This was the first person I had ever met who I recognized myself in.

On one of my days off I went up to Bradford and went to the Samaritans and said, 'Look, I gotta sort myself out, I don't know whether I'm a lesbian, I don't know whether I want a sex change, I don't . . . I have no fucking idea.' They gave me some stuff on CHE, the Campaign for Homosexual Equality, which I took away with me and had in my room. Now, what happened then was that I managed to speak to this particular person — whose name I've forgotten, but I can see her — him — so distinctly . . . um, and we had twenty minutes, and I said, 'Basically, I think I'm like you, I think I'm really a man inside.' And what she actually said was 'Don't do what I've done. Don't not do anything about it, I can't really talk to you about this but you need to get yourself sorted out, because this is an awful way of living.' And that was like a huge boot up the backside . . . and then, y'know, we talked for ten minutes . . . twenty minutes . . . and then she said, 'I can't talk to you about this any longer,' and went. I don't know whether it had anything to do with that, but two days later the housekeeper came down, having found the information sheets on the Campaign for Homosexual Equality in my room . . . Well, they obviously thought I was a lesbian and they'd had enough of those already, if you see what I mean.

Despite meeting the she-man, Stephen remained confused about his own nature, and after having literature about gay rights found in his room, he lost his job. An unsettled period followed, during which, thinking that his orientation was lesbian, he enlisted in the Army, then he decamped to Liverpool. It was by now 1974, and Stephen got a job at the council, in the Housing Department, and began to meet people associated with both the Women's Liberation Movement and the Campaign for Homosexual Equality.

There was a girl in the office, Shirley, she said, 'Where are you from?' So I told her, Manchester. 'Where are you living then?' I said, 'Well, I haven't got anywhere at the moment, my stuff's over at my mum's up there.' And she said, 'Well, you can come and stay with me.' So I went and stayed with her for a couple of nights. She thought I was a lesbian, introduced me to a friend of hers, Maureen, who was a lesbian, and I went to stay in Maureen's house in St Helens. Maureen was into a lesbian group at that point, in Manchester, so I used to come over to Manchester and go to the meetings for the Campaign for Homosexual Equality as a lesbian. I went to CHE for a while but couldn't deal with their politics, which were all about assimilation, and even then I knew I wasn't an assimilationist. GLF (Gay Liberation Front) started meeting at the Turk's Head in Manchester, so I went along to their meetings, and there was a group of women there who set up a radical lesbian separatist collective, and I thought, Well, that's more akin to my politics. And we got involved in setting up a women's centre here in Manchester.

And I went, late that summer, '74, to the last Women's Liberation Conference. It was held up in Edinburgh, and at that conference there was a huge debate going on about in what way women had to be women. They identified women as lesbians and separatists. So, this was this real problem for me, I remember standing up there saying, 'It's a real problem for me, y'know, we're all here consciousness-raising, talking about how we feel, the trouble is, well, I feel like I'm a man.' And you've never seen so much shit hit the fan in your life! People were thumping each other . . . I was stood up right in the middle of it, it was like a school hall where you all sat on the floor . . . I remember some of the women from the collective grabbing me and charging me out of the place before I got beat up.

What really appealed to me about women's politics was the idea that biology wasn't destiny. It struck me immediately as how I felt and where I belonged. I got involved with this lesbian collective and we set up a women's centre here in Manchester, at that time as a refuge for battered women. It was an old property which was falling to bits around everybody's heads. We did all sorts of work – I mean we did everything. It was every single aspect of it, from putting together beds to laying carpets – it was all absolute quality provision!

Jeans and sweatshirts, that's what I liked about working for the Housing Department – I was manifesting myself as if I were a lesbian. Actually, nobody gave a toss what I wore, I was so low down the pecking scale – as long as I filled in the forms!

Shirley's husband and I had this whole discussion about bisexuality around this time. He was basically making a pass at me. She had a child with somebody else, and yes, they sometimes slept together and they sometimes slept with other people. They got on well together and lived together, it was very much an alternative family. But we had this whole discussion about bisexuality and it occurred to me this was a label that I could understand. Being a lesbian was not right for me because, y'know, the women I'd tried to sleep with – it had been an absolute disaster. Being bisexual was a much easier place to position myself.

When we came back from the Women's Liberation Conference, we were crashing on somebody's floor in Manchester, and we were sort of sat round, and I said, 'Y'know, I think I've got a real problem on my hands, in fact, I know I want to have a sex change.' I mean, you're talking about the seventies, so our language was very, very restricted at that time. There weren't words to describe how you felt. I mean, I couldn't explain. There was no such notion as transgender, 'transsexual' was a word that rarely appeared. What people had was sex changes. I went to see *Boys Don't Cry* the other night. I was watching it, and at one point the character played by Hilary Swank is asked by a policeman, 'What's going on?' And he says, 'I've got a sexual identity crisis.' And I thought, Yes, this is how we termed it.

This was 'a sexual identity crisis'. Because you were either straight, or you were a lesbian, or you were a gay man; you might be bisexual, but bisexuals were just greedy people who wanted to sleep with anybody, any old time. And you were a man or you were a woman. You could only be positioned where everybody else put you. I remember at the time thinking a lot that all of the things, all of the language we used in the way we talked about issues, was far too restrictive. I still find that now. When I teach gender issues – I teach on a masters course in psychosexual therapy, I do stuff on gender – I'm trying to get these very experienced nurses to just move beyond the binary, not to fall into binary traps immediately. Y'know: let's try and reconceptualize this; can we think of any other way of talking about it? But of course, what they do is they talk about it in the same language framework all the time.

But I had this experience where I told these women how I felt. We crashed out at their place, and I explained how I felt and that I thought I was a man really, and I didn't know what to do, and I had to leave the collective, it was all beyond me – and they were just brilliant. The two women whose flat it was, one of them, Maggie, went off and got a jacket and a tie out of the wardrobe, and they talked about it and they took me to a club out in Ashton, the other side of Manchester, to meet somebody, and it was a transsexual woman, Carole, male to female. I'd seen her before and I'd just presumed that she was a woman. She was pre-op; she was still living and working in her male role during the day but going out as Carole at night. So in many ways she provided a sort of mechanism for how the change could work: you could actually live a double life for a while.

And we talked, we talked that night; the following night we met up again and Carole introduced me to a couple of other people, Stan, who was a transvestite, and Linda, his partner, who was a male-to-female transsexual. Those three and me, and another chap, Roy, who had a house in Camp Street in Salford, we set up what was basically the very first self-help group for transsexuals and transvestites in this country – it was so appropriate that they lived in Camp Street! It was 1974, and we used to meet there, and we set up the Manchester TV/TS Group.

We began publicizing the Group, but we were doing stickers on toilets in Manchester, that sort of CHE method. I remember us advertising in the *Gay Times* – well, it was the *Gay News* then. We found an organization called the Beaumont Society, which was the TV group, and we put adverts in their newsletter, and we got a room in the local university chaplaincy, and people could change there, that was what was really good about that. It turned out my old scripture teacher was married to the chaplain and she was totally cool about it!

It must have been about May, I got a job in Manchester, working for an insurance company as a clerk. So I moved back, got a room, and at that point I was going out in the evenings as Peter. I went to work in my female role, albeit barely – still in jeans and sweatshirt. I managed to get another job at that point, working as a technician, so again I was wearing jeans and sweatshirts, but I was, like, Peter in the rest of my life. At that point I became Stephen. It was February 1975 that I changed my name. We were going out to the Beaumont Society annual dinner in London, and everybody else said that 'Peter' was too old fashioned and staid, and they went through the alphabet and chose 'Stephen'.

I remember thinking at the time that I didn't mind being called Stephen if everybody else was happy to call me Stephen, and if it meant that I was a bloke, that was fine. What they said was they felt 'Peter' was not a name they could use. It didn't fit with my age and things like that, so it just didn't jell, but 'Stephen', every second guy in Manchester is called Steve or Stephen – as I've long discovered. So they were absolutely right, they picked something I've just blended in with.

I met an interesting couple called Brooklyn and Layla around this time. I'd seen an advert in *Gay News* for TAO (Transsexual Action Organization) and had written to them. Brooklyn and Layla lived in a bedsit in Birmingham; Brooklyn was a female-to-male transsexual and Layla was a male-to-female transsexual. They were living as a couple, sleeping together, having sex together and having this radical new approach. It was Layla who first helped me bind my chest, bound my chest till my fingers went blue! They came to Manchester for the weekend and took me out to the Oxfam shop, and I bought a jacket, trousers and tie – that was it. I used to go down to Birmingham and crash out on their floor. We did our own personal protest against the National Front Rally one weekend. TAO was – it's ironic really – so radical and way out, long before its time. A really radical new approach to living, a new way of being completely, and a coining of our demands, which were surgery on demand; hormones on demand; that we weren't mentally ill; that we were the gender we said we were; that gender roles didn't really exist, they were just a tool of the oppressive patriarchy – and so on and so forth. Good for '74.

The minute I started to socialize as Peter, the depression lifted. It was March when I finally started to go to work as Stephen – and, I mean, that was just a huge difference, that was like the point where I wasn't going to kill myself any longer – that step of doing it; and it was difficult because the radical transsexual movement at that point was fairly new.

At that point I started a relationship with somebody called Pat, who was a male-to-female transsexual. She'd set up the London TV/TS Group, and we lived together for a couple of years – I mean, the relationship probably lasted nine months, but we still keep in touch to this day. She's not been involved on the scene for twenty years, whereas I carried on. That relationship made me really address the issues about sex and sexual orientation, because I was having a relationship with someone who was biologically male, and I was biologically female and yet to the outside world I was the bloke and she was the woman.

At this time I was very, very androgynous. I mean, sometimes I passed and sometimes I didn't. From June '74 through to December '75, how people viewed me was very variable. I didn't actually start hormones until the end of May '75, so I'd been living as Stephen for three to four months when I started, so I'd been going to work as Stephen with no treatment whatsoever, to a workplace where everybody knew my past. I had a boss at work who was really good, and one day he asked me, 'What the fuck's wrong with you? You're going to lose your job, because you're never in on time.' Partly, I was going out clubbing to meet people. So I was out till four or five in the morning and then I'd have to be at work for eight o'clock.

I felt very vulnerable, incredibly vulnerable. Very frightened a lot of the time, of being read. I wasn't sure what I was actually frightened of. I found that starting to live as Stephen was very difficult, because I'd had relationships with men before but, suddenly, of course, they were an absolute no-no; and then I also felt incredibly vulnerable around them. I was really worried about how I was going to be seen; if they saw that I was female, what about sexual assault and suchlike? The whole thing was in many ways terrifying. Really, really, really terrifying.

In work and in general, I mean, nowadays I'm not bothered at all, but I had a long period when I was very much treading a fine line between being out and being in – a long period of life where I was out in some circumstances and very closeted in others. But there was no learning. People have always said that to me, 'How did you learn anything?' I didn't learn a thing. It just happened. Suddenly I fitted in. I was just able to be me. I didn't have to practise anything, the only things I had to learn was how do you shift from jeans and sweatshirts female mode to jeans and sweatshirts male mode? And there were very little subtle things, like always wear a belt on your trousers. I've got small feet, and shopping for shoes was a huge, major task. How do you get shoes that look like grown-up men's shoes but are small? So there were those sorts of things, and I always remember somebody at work saying to me – 'cos this was the 70s and everybody had their hair down to here – 'Stephen, just cut your hair off, it'll make a big difference. Just make that change, before you start the course, just cut your hair off, get it removed.'

My next relationship was with another male-to-female transsexual; I slept with several other male-to-female transsexuals, on trips and things like that. I didn't actually have a relationship with an RG, as they were called – a 'real girl' – until I met Sarah, which was quite a lot later, when I was twenty-two. I only slept with transsexuals, and I had a couple of sexual experiences with men, which were OK, but I sort of stayed within the transsexual world in terms of relationships, which in itself was hard, because even when I got to the point when I could pass, they couldn't necessarily pass. That's had a huge impact on why I continued around the scene. I became really incredibly aware that passing was a great privilege. It was a privilege afforded to a few of us . . . and most of my community, most of the people I loved, enjoyed the company of, could have the same crack with – just didn't have that privilege.

Six months into taking the hormones I realized that I was going to be OK. But other people who I cared about were not going to be OK. The fact is that Alex, Nick, Brooklyn, Paul and I, we could all swagger off somewhere, we could be guys out together. It would mean binding our chests and being a bit uncomfortable, but nobody was going to say anything; we were just this little men's convention. But our girlfriends – and Paul, Nick, Brooklyn, myself, we all had relationships with male-to-female transsexuals at this point – couldn't pass. So we were constantly putting ourselves into situations where we were going out with people who didn't pass or who were vulnerable. They were the ones who were being insulted in the street, we were the ones potentially throwing the fists.

I admit, I still find it difficult, on occasions, to publicly present myself as part of the transsexual community. I'm much more 'don't give a toss', but I'm very aware that my mother would say, 'Well, I don't know why you're mixing with those people still!' Fortunately, there have been enough people who've stayed around. I and a few others have been around the longest, and I don't know whether we're just stupid or idealistic. A lot of people hang around for quite a period – particularly people who're involved in group organization and the politics – but most of them reach a point and say, 'Look I want to move on in my life, I want to forget that this is there.'

I found the new relationships I began having with male-to-female transsexuals incredibly comfortable. I mean, this was me, as a man, having a relationship with a woman. Forensically, we would have been perceived as being a straight couple, both of whom were cross-dressers. So, what you had was, all the bits and bobs were the wrong bits and bobs – they'd been given to the wrong people. But you actually felt really comfortable with having that body. I mean, all of us were aspiring to having our bodies sorted out, but we could live with the other person, because the other person said, 'You think your body's a problem? You should see my body!' Before, if I'd been in bed with a woman, prior to my living as Stephen, the trouble was she always wanted somebody who I wasn't. And I found it very difficult to say, 'Hold on a minute, that's not me, this is who I am.'

Of course, I kept away from RGs because I was terrified of being in big trouble. There were girls that I knew and fancied but just didn't get involved with 'cos I thought, Oh, shit what's her mother going to say when she finds out? And that was a mental precursor to exactly what did happen.

In '74, when we set up the TV/TS Group, I'd gone to my GP and said, I want to go and see a specialist in this area, I want a sex change. She sent me to see a psychiatrist in Manchester's Withington Hospital, who was an arrogant little toad! I went to see him several times. I told him that I wanted to have hormone treatment, I didn't think I was mad. I said to him, 'I'm not stupid, I did biology O Level, I know that I'm physically female, everything works and is perfectly normal, but that's not me and I know that having a sex change is possible, and I want it, and I want hormone treatment . . . and so on and so forth. So, he sent me off to see the psychologist, who was a very strange man, who had a huge big cyst on the top of his bald head, so it was virtually impossible to concentrate on any psychology in the middle of it all. But it was a really bizarre system: I always remember he had photographs of people from the 1950s, and you'd have to say who was more attractive, the male characters or the female characters.

They finally sent me to see a psychologist – a young woman. We sat and chatted for about forty minutes, and then I was meant to go and see her once a week for six months. On the first occasion, I sat there, and after forty minutes she said, 'Well, this is a waste of time.' And I thought she was going to say, 'That's it, I'm not bothering to see you.' But she said, 'It strikes me that you're perfectly sane, you perfectly and absolutely know what you want to do. I can't see any reason for you not to do it, I think you'd be terribly successful, I'll write a letter.' And she wrote the letter in front of me. We didn't hear anything for a while, so I got my GP to chase up the psychiatrist. Eventually I got an appointment and went down to see him again. He just said, 'I won't treat you, you will never, ever, ever make it as a man. Absolutely not, and you'll get nothing out of the National Health Service.'

That must have been May '75, because I had actually been working as Stephen for three months. So I couldn't change my name back. I mean, what the fuck was I meant to do now? I'd changed my name, I'm living as a bloke, I'm working as a bloke, I'm shagging as a bloke and they wanted me to stop it? Jesus Christ, you'd think that changing one way was bad enough, for fuck's sake!

I knew people who were already having treatment. The generation prior to me had not had it easy. They got all of the crap, ended up having a year or two in a locked ward on a psychiatric unit. I think I was really lucky that I was part of the first generation to come through without that, thank God. But when I got knocked back, I went home with the full intention of doing myself in. I was still living with Pat, I knew she'd still be at work, and I went home to kill myself. And my GP was actually sat on the doorstep, and she said, 'I know what he's said, I've had a letter from him, and I'm going to write you out a prescription for hormones.' She was an amazing woman. She got in big trouble for it. I gather she lost her job in the end, she was barred from working for two years in England. We've kept in touch since, and she was just the most impressive character. She just knew that I was going to do it. She also knew there were ways of giving people positive lives and making sure they don't kill themselves.

So I went to the chemist, got the hormones and started to take them. The initial relief was just astonishing. Just to think, This is it – it's starting. I knew what would happen, but I didn't know how quickly. The stuff that we took then was a pill you stuck under your tongue four or five times a day and let dissolve. It was a dreadful bore because it took nearly an hour! But I was really lucky, within six weeks my voice started to break, and my whole body shape began to change within a few months. At the end of a year I was starting to grow a beard. But it took me ten years to grow a moustache. For a long time I just used to have one of these big Dutch beards, tons of it, and no moustache at all! I got hairy on my chest quickly, the whole thing, it was very quick, probably at the end of eighteen months nobody would've ever guessed.

The gradual relief of realizing the pattern was just easing – that was really very nice. A gradual move, because every time somebody said, 'Yes, madam?' your heart plummeted. There was also an awful period of having to tell people over and over and over again, 'Oh, I'm planning on having a sex change.'

I told my dad one evening when he was quite drunk. That was the only time that he ever talked to me about his wartime experiences. So, he rambled on a lot about landing on the beaches of Normandy and driving into Germany in a tank at the age of fifteen or sixteen. I had a great deal of respect for him at that point. And he said he would be totally supportive, wonderful! But he never was. I think he was a man who wanted to love us, he was just pretty lousy at it.

The first time he reneged was about six months later. My sister was having a Christmas party, and I was invited as Stephen. There was a very nice girl there, who I danced with. I didn't intend to do anything at all, but I flirted. So, my dad took her into one of the rooms and said, 'I'd better tell you about him, he's not what he seems. I was told at the party that she'd gone home. 'Why?' 'Dad's just told her.' 'Told her what? Oh, fucking shit! I wasn't going to do anything, it was a party, we were having a nice time.'

That attitude went on and on and on, to the point where the last fifteen years I barely spoke to him. I mean, right up to before he died he was calling me by my old name – even to my siblings.

But I didn't know how to be angry with anybody during all of this – I really didn't. I felt so bad, I felt so ashamed of what I was doing, I felt like I was the real failure. And I still, to this day, find it very hard to be angry with other people's attitudes about what I've done, because I always feel that it's my fault. In terms of gut feeling and how I feel about myself, I feel it to be a failure. In terms of what I know about myself it's a completely different kettle of fish. But in terms of the anxieties and the dreams that you have – it's me who fails, it's me who can't hack it.

Yet it's who I'm meant to me. At the beginning I felt that I didn't want to be in Manchester, but running away was not a solution. I'd seen other people's lives enough; been around the scene, not that long, but I'd seen enough of people's lives to realize that they were completely fucking isolated. They had no relatives, they had no friends, they didn't tell anybody, they didn't do anything.

I told my mother a couple of days after my father. She cried and said she had thought I was a lesbian, and this was very difficult . . . But she never lost contact over the next few months. She kept in touch by phone, and she'd cry on the other end about, 'Oh, this is going to be so difficult' and 'What will everybody think?' and 'How am I meant to tell everybody?' It was always 'What will the neighbours think?'

First of all, she'd come round to my flat – where I lived with Pat and Alex – and she'd sit there crying on the sofa for most of three hours, and one day Alex just said, 'I've had enough, Barbara. You're in our house, actually this is Stephen's place, this. You're sitting here, you're saying you don't like what he's doing. Well, if you don't like what he's doing just go away.' I'd never ever have dreamt of saying it to her, I couldn't have said it. He said, 'Just go home, go on the bus and go away, 'cos I'm sick of this happening once a fortnight, every second bloody Sunday. You come in here crying about what he's doing and you're in his place. When we go to your place we're perfectly civilized and we behave like grown-ups.'

So she put on her coat and went off to get the bus. And I said, 'I just can't do this to my mother.' And he said, 'Well, we could go out and get her back, and we could say that she's got to stop crying.' So I went out to the bus stop with him and said, 'Come back, but you've got to stop crying, tea's on.' And she said, 'OK, I'll stop crying.' And I'll give her her dues she's never cried since. If she has – she's cried away from me.

She's tried very hard to be very supportive – but at times she's found things very difficult. I always remember my twenty-first birthday. We were still living at the flat then, and she turned up with her friend Lucy. The flat was at the top of a house, and there were very camp gay men living on the floors below. We had this wild party, and she came along, and she and Lucy just let rip, really enjoyed it. So she really tried to join in with the community. She's always been incredibly welcoming to community members. If we have an occasion and I ask for beds for people, she always takes them in. She spends hours talking to people on the phone. She still says, 'I don't understand it. I've no idea how Stephen feels, I can't even fathom for a minute.'

Yet she relates to me completely as a son. She's said the thing she found most difficult was moving from saying she had three girls and two boys to saying she had two girls and three boys. I remember when my nan died – her mum – we were stood at the funeral and somebody said, 'But Barbara, didn't you have three girls?' And my mum said, 'No, don't be so daft.' And I could see that she was killing herself laughing at the same time. Finally she's managed to break out of 'this is the most awful event of my life' to 'really, this is quite funny: "No, of course I've always had two daughters and three boys!"' And she was just killing herself at the time.

She found it very difficult when we were having our first baby. She didn't say anything to us, but my sister said she had a blazing row with her, 'cos my mother was sitting knitting something, and Patricia said, 'Oh, is that for Sarah's baby?' And she said, 'Oh, I don't know about that. I don't know whether I approve of any of this.' And Patricia just said, 'Oh, for God's sake, you know at least it's a baby that's bloody wanted!'

My mum's behaviour towards the kids has always been impeccable, she's never questioned our lifestyle and what we do. She's always been totally supportive. She may have her doubts, but those are things she voices elsewhere to other people. She's very popular in the family's church, and I think the very fact that she gets an immense amount of support has been important. It's the same church that I went to as a child, yet people there say, 'You must be so proud of your Stephen, he's achieved such a lot. He and Sarah have done so well, they've got such lovely kids.' I'm one of the people that they, as a community, are proud of, and therefore my mother's proud of me as well.

What it's done, over the years, is make me feel that not being out about one's transsexual status is the biggest mistake that you could make. It really doesn't make you any less of a man or a woman and in fact the benefits far outweigh the disadvantages. I mean, I was doing somebody's case the other week, his partner is applying for fertility treatment at a clinic and one of the things the clinic had said was that they were very concerned about giving them treatment as a couple, because everybody in their local neighbourhood knows that Alan's not a real bloke. So they're saying, 'Well, perhaps if you moved areas . . .', and I'm saying to these people, 'They're fucking crazy to think that. Actually, as a family, you'll get far more support, because everybody does know you've had to fight a bit harder; and why the fuck should you have to pretend it's not happened?'

My sister Christine – well, she hasn't been perfect, but she was a social worker, so she's tried very hard to do her best, even if at times, particularly at the beginning, she fucked up. As for my other siblings, Patricia was interesting 'cos we'd always hated each other. We had shared a bedroom and she'd been the one with the really messy dressing-table I couldn't stand. It took us a while, two or three years, but actually we've become best friends. She just said, 'Whatever, whatever you want to do, it's fine by me.' I think partly it's because she's had a life-threatening illness that she's been all right. And then, when Patricia had her second baby, he died at sixteen weeks. I was working up in Bolton at the time – this was in the early eighties – and I used to drive past the hospital on my way home, so I used to go in so that Patricia could be with her daughter for two or three hours, and I stayed with Christopher. And the very fact that I'd been there every night, it was an experience that we both had together. But even before that, whatever we are, each of us, we class each other as best friends. We just had no chance when we were kids.

As for my brothers, Alan's always been away. He went down to the Imperial (Imperial College, London) and then went and did a post-doctorate in the States. He now works down in a chemical company, and we get on fine. He's cool, he's laid back. He's a hardened socialist and lives with his partner. No kids, but that's just his life. He's a chemist, makes rat poison which he's going to save the world with. As far as he's concerned – I'm his brother. We get on fine, he likes my kids, he likes the fact that I lead an alternative life, and keeps on saying, 'I'm really looking forward to you becoming a professor one day, just so that I can say I've got a brother who is a professor.'

My other brother, Malcolm, was much more difficult. He was the youngest. He was in the Merchant Navy when I changed over, and was coming back and forth from sea. When I moved down to Brighton in 1977, he was going to college in London. He didn't know anybody down south, so he used to drive down on his motorbike with his mates and crash out on my floor, really so as not to be in the college, or naval barracks, or whatever they were. And we had a couple of tense occasions; I mean, I can always remember him sitting down – and I have completely forgiven him – but I remember at the time thinking how on earth can I ever forgive him? 'Cos one of the things that he said was, 'Oh, I can remember sitting at home and saying, "Well, really it would have been better if you'd killed yourself."' And then he said, 'I think in retrospect I still probably do think that.' But he was only twenty-one or something.

And he also said, 'I still think it was just too difficult for us as a family and it's still too awkward.' Then we had a spate of working together for a while in the mid-eighties. I'd walked out of a job 'cos the situation was very difficult, Malcolm had left the Navy. He set up a business which I invested my savings in, and he also wanted somebody who could do the books. We worked with somebody else, who I hadn't told my past to. Malcolm told him one night in the pub, and the other guy pulled out of the business and I lost all my money.

But the reality is we come from a large family, we've got to see each other on occasions, whether we like it or not. I said, 'I could tell you to fuck off, but that means that every time there's a family do, one of us will have to walk out of the room.' So, he's screwed up enough as it is. I remember saying to people, 'He's just who he is, it's his own loss. There will be jobs, but the business has gone. Do I have to spend the rest of my life thinking that every time there's a family do, people are wondering whether to invite me or him?'

Malcolm still finds it really hard. He finds it very difficult to have to deal with this weird person in his family. He's so straight and conformist. He runs his own business, a big engineering firm. He lives up in Bolton, which is so fucking straight it's unbelievable. I had to drive up there for something the other week, and I stopped at a Little Chef for a cup of coffee, and I realized that the place was full of men in grey suits and white shirts and grey ties – this is still what this place is about.

I think, for Malcolm, family is very important – and the sense of belonging to a family still. I do find it difficult, I mean, like when my dad died, it never occurred to me that there'd be any other situation but Alan and Malcolm as pallbearers. They couldn't have stood the idea of me being a pallbearer. Malcolm, particularly, would never have been able to tolerate that idea. But in many ways I felt like saying, 'But I'm entitled.' I'm not going to say that though. Because I think my feeling is one of, I'm always gonna be an outsider, I'm always gonna be different, I'm always gonna be weird to you. It's hard to explain but it feels like you're getting into trouble. I remember the sensation of being a kid, thinking, Fuck, when I get home I'm gonna be in trouble! And that's always, always lingering. A few weeks ago I drove out to my sister's to pick up two of my kids who had stayed there overnight. It was a Saturday lunchtime, and I had a pair of tie-dyed surfing bottoms on and a T-shirt. I was driving along, and I thought, It's Saturday lunchtime and my dad's gonna be there. Oh fuck! I know what he'll say, 'Oh what the fuck are you wearing, oh, what do you call those? Ugh!' It's always about What're you wearing, why aren't you wearing clothes like everybody else is meant to wear? My mother still does this a bit. Y'know, it's all about making sure you blend in and making sure you're not in any way, shape or form seen to be different. And it was an almighty relief to realize that my father was dead and he wasn't going to be there. He wasn't going to be there and he wasn't going to say it and I could wear the fucking trousers.

It was really interesting living as a bloke and beginning the hormones. For a start, I looked considerably younger than I was. Instead of being a nineteen- or twenty-year-old, I now looked like a thirteen- or fourteen-year-old. And then there was this absolute shift: instead of being 'love' or 'duck' – which they call women in Manchester – I suddenly became 'son'.

And to most men I was, literally, little. Right the way through to my mid-thirties I always appeared much younger than I was.

On top of that, I had this experience of re-becoming somebody, of re-embodying myself. It was like being a child, it really was. I'm trying to think back to the experience of binding. The first time we bound my chest, I went out with Brooklyn and Layla, out round the shops in Moss Side, and we bought a jacket from Oxfam. There was this incredible experience of not knowing how it worked. As I said before, lots of people have asked me, 'Well, did you practise being a man?' Well, no, of course I didn't practise being a man. I didn't know what the hell to practise for a start – I had no experience. And taking the hormones, there was this huge testosterone rush, which meant I became incredibly orientated towards sex.

The whole of my waking life I was thinking about sex. I always used to joke about the places that I've masturbated in, but, y'know, it wasn't a joke – it was real. It was this pervading sex thing, but at the same time sex was very complicated, too, because I had this female body. At the very beginning I had this female body and this really incredibly strong sex drive, and on top of that, a hunger for food that was unbelievable, and this incredible sensation of aggression that came with it. So, there were three factors that I had to deal with. But having the entirely female body, which I was trying to manipulate and hide, was combined with trying to deal with these extra things that I'd never experienced before. It was odd, because I'd been incredibly aggressive as a girl; I'd been somebody who on one level was always threatening to lose control, and at the same time I was considered a mardy baby because I cried about things. Then, when I took testosterone all the crying about things disappeared very quickly and I've rarely cried since.

There was a steady undercurrent of all the time feeling angry and, I mean, that was probably for about two years; it was the only time I was ever angry about the fact that I was transsexual. I felt so cheated – and I was angry that I had to live in a world in which I was so alienated. It's that sort of experience that's the precursor to who I am today, because I'd always been a political creature from when I was very young, in terms of thinking the philosophy of how we existed had to be addressed, and that most of the way people lived was completely at odds with what we should be doing. So that combined with this experience.

I can always remember my dad saying when I was about seventeen, 'Oh, well, of course you're really angry now.' I had a picture of Lenin somewhere. 'You're seventeen, but by the time you're twenty-five you won't be angry at all, nobody ever is.' But by the time I was twenty-five I was angrier than ever, and in one sense that anger has grown and grown. How I deal with this has developed in a different way, but I'm much angrier now than I ever was. I may not appear it, but my anger at the world and the way systems work is just overwhelming, it pervades my daily existence.

When it came to taking hormones, well, I'd met another couple of female-to-male transsexuals, but we were so rare on the ground that we didn't really, sort of, exist, so nobody told me what to expect in any way, shape or form. Not at all. I mean, at that point I knew hardly anybody who'd ever had the therapy. I'd met Nick, who'd transitioned when he was about fourteen, and so he'd been very young, but he'd had hormones when he was eighteen, so at that point he was seven or eight years older than me and had been through it for quite a long period. It never occurred to him to warn me.

Mostly, the relief was tremendous – the feeling of actually progressing, of moving forwards, of knowing that I could actually live and have a life. But at the same time there was sheer horror about what I was doing – I mean, I was setting myself so far apart from society that I felt I was almost like a figure scurrying around in dark alleys. At that time that's what I felt my life consisted of; I wasn't anybody in anyone's life – except in the secret world of transsexuals. And I'd sort of flip in and out of their lives, and I wasn't actually a real human being then, I wasn't ever going to form relationships with other human beings. So, I had this feeling of all this; the effects were just fabulous – but really alien.

I had a horrendous experience in the middle of all this. I'd probably been on hormones for about three or four months, and cycling home from work on my bike I had the most horrendous stomach cramps, and then I got home and I sat on the toilet and I passed very large clots of blood. Of course, that meant I had to go to hospital. And by then I was passing as a bloke. I remember ringing up Nick and saying, 'I just don't know what to do', and he said, 'We should get you to the hospital.' I went to the hospital and they treated me with utter disdain. It was, 'Well, you're taking this crap, what the hell do you expect? We'd like that bed in an hour – I think you can go now.' I carried on passing clots of blood for another twenty-four hours, thinking, I can't go to work, and if I don't go to work I don't have enough money. I can't explain to anybody – I mean, I've never been able to explain to anybody – the horror of having to go to the hospital and explain who I am; of having to say, 'My name is Stephen Whittle, and I'm passing blood, and this is where I'm passing blood from.'

It was never explained to me what was happening, but that was the last period I ever had, if you can call it a period. I'd not actually had anything for about ten or twelve weeks at that point, and then I'd passed these huge clots, which were the size of my fist. And that moment of knowing that I had to go to the hospital, and I had to explain this, had to sit in Casualty, where there were people in the cubicles next to you, and explain this whole story – in many ways it sums up the awfulness of what I was going through: that I felt neither man nor woman. I felt like a piece of shit. I felt like a monster creature.

But I never doubted my sanity. I always knew, right from being very young, that I was sane – I could work it out for myself and I knew exactly who I was. And I knew what I needed to do in order to live. People often say to me, 'Oh, well, did you know you were a man?' But it wasn't that easy. What I knew was that in order to live I had to live as a man; being a man meant that I could do the things I had to do in my life in order to live. And that was everything, from eating meals to going to work to having relationships; from buying a house to riding a bike.

There was a two to three year period when these things were gradually taking place; and I was very lucky that I started to grow a beard within a year, and my voice broke very quickly, and my body shape changed, but the most difficult thing to deal with was that I still had breasts. Within a fairly short space of time, a year or so, they didn't look like ordinary women's breasts, they were different. They'd lost shape to them; they hadn't reduced in size as such, but they were easier to bind and, in part, the binding made a difference to the shape. Then, in the course of eighteen months, I developed chest hair. So I had this peculiar body, which was quite hairy, but was technically female, and it didn't look like a woman's body at all. It looked like something completely different. I can remember thinking, How would I describe myself? If I was giving a name to this, what would I call it? You can, after all, call a dog a dog.

But I was much happier once I started to grow hair – much, much happier with my body. I began to enjoy my arms, and I started going to the gym, and I enjoyed my legs, and I felt my genitals and my chest were my only difficult pieces. Although I'd been involved in the women's movement, and they'd all done that radical gynaecology thing where people should look at their bits, I'd obviously avoided that like the plague. I probably didn't look at my genitals until about two years ago, and then it was only for health reasons. I would avoid them. They were – and they still are to a large extent – almost a reminder of not being a human being. And that's very difficult, because in theory terms it doesn't jell, because I know I'm a human being. In fact, I think I'm a pretty decent human being.

But, at the same time, it's not like being disabled, because a disability is something that makes a difference to you. This was almost like a decision, a *choice* to be different. After all, why couldn't I just dye my hair red to be different? But instead I chose this. And I was really torn for a long time: did I want a penis? Yet I don't think that was ever a major part of my agenda; it's difficult, I would like to have a penis simply for the intimacy of being joined with Sarah in sex, but the penis was never the major issue. When I went on testosterone my sex life was through the roof, but then I did think, Well, if I had the choice . . . the option of having a penis, would I? Because to do so would mean I'd look weird again – I'd read the stuff. And I realized to do so – certainly at that point – meant I'd probably lose all sexual sensation, and I didn't want that.

One night in 1974 or '75, I went to the Beaumont Society dinner dance, and I met Alice, who was a member. She was a male-to-female transsexual, who was still living as Anthony. She was still living, in fact, married, with kids. I met her as Alice – and just fell head over heels. From the word go we were having quite good sex. It was non-penetrative sex, and it was sex in which she was content to let me be the man. But it was still quite difficult, because she was quite a lot older than me, and I felt very much like a child in this, she was a very much more assertive person. I always felt like the whole thing was a bit out of my control – it was about her needs not mine.

In 1977 I moved down to Sussex and went to Sussex University. I wanted to go as 'Stephen'. I went through the application process and everything as 'Stephen'. But when I got there, the first thing that happened was that the dean called me in and said, 'I just want to check something over with you, Stephen. It says here that you went to Withington School. Well, I come from Manchester . . .' Oh shit! I had to admit that, yes, I went to Withington Girls' School, and yes, I'd had a sex change, y'know, and what's it to do with you? But of course, he didn't keep his trap shut. So quite a few people got to know fairly quickly. I moved to Brighton, into a bedsit, and I lived close to Alice, and we had an ongoing affair. But it became very obvious to me quite quickly that (a) she was not going to be the partner for me, and (b) she certainly was not going to give up her house and her lifestyle for me. She did ultimately transition after having surgery, but I knew that it was never going to be for me. Then, on top of that, I was also aware that this was somebody I could never ever live with – I mean, we would have killed each other.

So, I had this relationship with Alice, and I was at university. Initially I got on well. I mostly had women friends who I got on very well with. I ended up starting the second year and then taking the end of the second year off and then doing it again so I could get some space to cope with the jokes that were made about me. It was the jokes that I can remember most – and I just couldn't deal with that sort of thing, I needed space. At the same time I didn't want to give up; this was the point when I really started to think, Well, this is who I am, this is my starting place and, of course, this is where I began to grow up.

And, in fact, this is quite interesting, because I became, in effect, out, and various women from the university Women's Group there expressed sympathy about what had happened and they talked about my past, my history. I always remember, they decided to have this Christmas party, a women's Christmas party, and I was the person – the only man – allowed to go. And I went to that and I thought, Yeah, I belong here, too. Some bit of me belongs in here. I belong here, far better than down the pub with the lads, where I felt I was like a complete and utter alien. They were sexist, racist bigots. I wasn't interested. And once they'd had one drink too many, they were even worse sexist, racist bigots. Even at Sussex – and this was the place where in 1978 the whole university wore blue jeans on Blue Jeans be Gay for a Day Day. But it wasn't quite there yet, there was still the rugby element, there was still the 'this is what men do' business.

I can remember, we went on a field trip and some of the lads kidnapped – or lambnapped – a sheep, and carted it through the hotel; and at one point it ran through my bedroom and I was fucking blazing. Not because they'd done it to me, but because not one of them had seen the effect on the sheep. Y'know, this animal was out of its mind with terror. We had this huge row over breakfast, where I threw coffee over somebody. I got into trouble for throwing the coffee! But it was nothing compared to what these arseholes had been doing.

Around 1977 to '78 I had massive anxiety attacks and that whole thing. I remember being carted off to hospital after collapsing. I ended up being in a locked ward in Charing Cross Hospital. Of course, I was taken to Charing Cross 'cos I was transsexual, and I was put in a locked ward belonging to the man who did all the transsexual patients; he was completely off his trolley. It was a horrendous week – just an unbelievable experience. One chap died while I was there.

My mastectomy – it's still detectable. But now, twenty years on, I'm very hairy, and the scars have reduced a great deal. People might think, he's had a slight accident or something like that. I had it tidied up about thirteen years after it was first done, as it wasn't that satisfactory, but it was the reality of it which was most satisfactory. Later that summer I was in the sea, bare chested.

I woke up, and I'd had a hysterectomy – they did the mastectomy and hysterectomy all at once – and I felt like Marley's ghost. Like I had these huge chains piled on top of me, and I was lying there going, 'Arghh! Fucking shit!' But still there was the utter, utter, utter sense of amazing relief. I didn't care what it looked like, it didn't matter any more, the bandages were off, the clothes were out and I was able to wear just a shirt. Before that I'd always worn a binder, a Lycra T-shirt, a shirt, probably a jumper or a jacket as well.

To begin with, it had been impossible to get the surgery. I couldn't get it at all. I couldn't get anybody to even consider it. Then, what happened was, in about May of that year [1978], I had some bleeding. Partly through taking hormones I had an erosion of the cervix which meant I had bleeding, and that was just beyond me . . . that was the point I really went off my head, because the only answer was to use sanitary towels. I'd've rather just bled down my leg, thank you. I really would have done. I'd rather have bled to death. And I went to see the GP, who had no idea what to do. He suggested the VD clinic! So, Sarah came along with me to the clinic, and we had a huge hoo-ha, because the doctor wanted to examine me, which meant putting my legs up in stirrups, which were, of course, round in the ladies' section. Anyway, they found I needed to have a hysterectomy. That's the only answer they had. It was dead straightforward: 'Stephen, you can have a hysterectomy, that's the only answer for it.' I said, 'That's fine.' And they said, 'When did you have your other surgery?' I said, 'I'm still fucking waiting.' And they replied, 'We'll get that done at the same time. You'll need to see a psychiatrist, can you arrange that?' and I said, 'Yeah, fine.'

Two weeks later we went to see a mad psychiatrist who mostly wanted to know what we did in bed and kept on asking us if we had group sex with people. He talked to Sarah alone at one point, and said, 'How many other relationships have you had?' And she said, 'Before I met Stephen, nothing big, no big deals, you know, after a party sort of thing.' And so he said, 'So how many women have you slept with altogether?' 'I haven't slept with any women.' 'But you've just told me you've had a few relationships.' I mean, that group-sex business, for Christ's sake, grow up! Just sign the paper! All he wanted was the sex bit, but it was none of his business.

But the initial doctor was a nice bloke. He didn't do the chest surgery himself, I went into Sussex County, and first of all he didn't appear, I was down there for hours and hours.

He was going to do the hysterectomy and somebody else was going to do the chest. He gave me the pre-med, and I said, 'I've not seen the surgeon who's going to do my chest. I really would like to talk to them before they do it.' I'd heard of people having dreadful scars and nobody had told me anything. I knew friends who'd got huge triangular holes in their chests; I knew that wasn't necessary and I just wanted to talk about it. But the ward sister came and said, 'You people, just a waste of bloody National Health Service money.' Eventually somebody came down and drew a few lines on me, and I was fine. At least they were talking to me, so they knew that I was interested in what the process was going to be. Then they took me down to surgery and I sat and waited and waited and waited.

About a year later a guy came up to me in the park said, 'Hello, I didn't recognize you.' It turned out he was the anaesthetist, and his girlfriend had been the theatre sister. Apparently there'd been one surgeon on either side of my chest, and one surgeon had started on the one side, but the other one went, 'Mm, I'm not very happy about this and I can't go ahead with it' (apparently for religious reasons). So the other surgeon went on and finished the one side, but then he left also – and by then I was losing blood and getting cold; they then spent four hours pounding round trying to find another surgeon to finish the job off.

Now this was 1978, and if you were transsexual you were still so far beyond the Pale . . . So, it wasn't a brilliant job really. Even when I got back home, the district nurse arrived and gave me a long lecture on how she wanted me to put my own dressings on because I was just a waste of National Health Service money, and why didn't I pay for it privately?

Just before I went into the hospital I'd been offered a job teaching English as a foreign language. It was to start just two weeks after I had the surgery. So, having a full hysterectomy and going back to work felt like shit for the first month, but I needed the job. But the utter sense of relief I had when I came home was amazing. OK, there were scars and it was bloody and everything, but I no longer had these breasts which I couldn't lie down without feeling. As I say, I've really got to like the bits – there's lots of bits about me I've got to like, but my breasts always gave me this huge sensation of making me not quite a human being.

I reckon it takes two years to get used to the testosterone, and then a few years after that to adjust it to what suits you. Once you've had a hysterectomy you've got to address it again, because you've lost all your baselines at that point, so you decrease the dose of testosterone. You've got to not take so much that you give yourself the risk of enhanced liver cancer; and not so little that you find yourself in a post-menopausal state of hot flushes all the time. Enough in order to have a good sex drive, but not so much that you're thinking about it all the time. It probably took about five or six years for me to get that balance right.

There was a good endocrinologist who helped me when we came back to Manchester. I'd go and meet him, and we'd um and ah and chat and try another approach. He'd say, 'Instead of taking that once a month try to take half of this once every two weeks – and then let's just do some blood tests to see what the levels are.' I went on to intramuscular injections after about two years; they were much better, had less possibility of side effects and were much more effective.

But all of those experiences on their own didn't matter so much to me. The key thing for my sense of identity was having this lifelong experience that came from my relationship with Sarah; it was in the relationship with her that I was able to shift from being just masculine to being a man. Then I became a whole human being, regardless of what state my body was in. You know, as far as she was concerned, I was a man. I could've been a man who was in a wheelchair, I could've been a man who was deaf, I could have been a man who'd lost his willy in an accident, it was simply that I was a transsexual man. From her I was able to come to terms with who I was and I decided it was possible to be just a man, but that included being able to be a transsexual man – and that was it absolutely and completely. I never asked Sarah whether at any point she had thought any differently about me, and I don't want to know. Because I felt it was her total acceptance that allowed me to be who I was. She then told everybody else, 'He is going to get on with his life, because it's not just his life any more – this is my life, too. And this is who we are going to be.'

I was thinking about my relationship with Sarah – and it's the first time I'd ever pieced it together – but that was such a crucial point for me. 'Growing up' is the wrong term – because growing up is something that's taken much longer. I mean, I'm very aware that I went through a sort of youth, again, so it was only in my forties that I thought – I'm grown up; I was able to feel grown up. But the relationship was a real step from being almost a nothing – an inadequate person – to actually being somebody, and that somebody was distinctly a man.

And that had nothing to do with the sex *per se*; it wasn't to do with money (we didn't have any), but it was a function of being regarded, by somebody else, as a whole human being, a complete and absolute human being, regardless of whatever shape my body was or anything like that. But this is who she saw. I'd always had this sensation of desperately wanting to grow up to be myself – whoever that was. And I couldn't envisage myself growing older and becoming someone everybody else expected to see. Then this person came along who saw who I was – and that was a 'man', a sort of man, whatever that means, because we're all sort of men – and that was distinctly me, and I knew who it was and that I could fit into it, and finally be.

The first time we slept together, we'd gone to a party, and I pointedly looked at her and said, 'Oh, who's coming to bed with me then?' She smiled back and said, 'I am.' And I remember thinking, 'Oh my God, this is terrifying.' And we went upstairs, and I said, 'I just can't take off my clothes.' And she was absolutely fine about it, but she said, 'You know, you're going to have to one day.' And over the next few months I had this realization that she didn't see my body as being any less, or any different – it was me. It was my body. It was entirely labelled by me. And I remember when I had my chest surgery, discussing it, and her saying, 'Well, of course you want your chest surgery and I'm totally behind you, but you do realize that it doesn't matter to me. It absolutely doesn't make an iota of difference to me whether you do or you don't, because you are just you.' But that just 'me' wasn't somebody weird – it wasn't essentially a transsexual person.

The relationship has eased things, but it's provided its own sense of guilt, because the repercussions in Sarah's life were phenomenal. She was ostracized and ousted by her parents, her life was torn apart. We were only speaking about it the other day, and she said, 'Well, I gave up everything for you.' And that's precisely what she did. She's obviously got lots back in one sense, but at that time she took this huge step of walking out of her life – and everything that had been planned. Her parents were journalists and worked for the BBC at various points, and the idea was that she'd go to Paris and get a trainee newsreader's job, go into journalism there, then come back. And all of this was completely lost – she jettisoned her middle-class upbringing. For a period of time she lost her parents – her father for thirteen years and her mum for about eleven.

There were odd bits of contact, and we always tried to behave in an exemplary manner. I wasn't allowed near their house or anything like that. On a couple of occasions I had to ring up Sarah's mother about things, and Sarah's father picked up the extension on one of these occasions, and he just said, 'Put that phone down!' And she had to put the phone down. Once Sarah went down for some occasion. They really wanted her to go, so I said, 'Look, just go, y'know, go and do it because this might be the way of finding a way through.' And she was very wary, but she did go, and then they kept her locked in her room for two days, while they just hounded her about being with me. She says now that what they did to her was horrendous in every single sense. Her father used to write letters saying that her mum had tried to kill herself.

Yet they're intrinsically liberal; they have gay friends, but this was too much. We often wonder whether Sarah's father would have hated his daughter going off with anybody, but I gave him the reason to hate not just me but the whole thing that I was, dragging her down to an appalling outsiders' level of society. A couple of times, Sarah's mother would say things like, 'Well, I can understand that Stephen's done it, but why do you still see him? And do you have to see other transsexual people? You know it's all very well, but some of them don't look very good!' Sarah would go up the bloody wall! The whole idea seemed to be that if this was going to be tolerated at all we had to fit in, to endeavour to be as middle class and as unnoticed as possible.

I never took this attitude — and I still think this — because while I may have all sorts of guilt, there's a strong political statement that I do believe, totally and completely, and this is: I've done nothing. I may have done things to myself, but what have I ever done to anybody else except endeavour to live my life as fully as possible, to participate as fully as possible, to be nice to people, as fully as possible? I mean, what more are you meant to do?

If there is guilt it's the guilt of actually choosing. Particularly now, the guilt is very much embodied through the fact that I have the body of a transsexual man, that I choose to have it and I choose to be out about it, and, further, that this constantly shakes other people's ground. I'm aware of this: I stand in a lecture and I teach, and for some people it's like an earthquake going on.

It provokes everything from tears of joy that, Thank God this world exists, to absolute horror. I've been accused of everything, ranging from being mad, to being bad, to being wicked, to being perverted. I always remember Sarah's mother watching some silly programme on telly a few years ago, and it was about mixed-religion and mixed-race marriages, and she said, 'I just don't understand this. I think the only thing I'd draw the line at is if one of my children went off with somebody who was into organized crime and murder and things like that.' And I said, 'Oh, that's really very interesting – what did I do? Which gang was I in?' And she could see it then and she could laugh. But the fact is that what I've done gets categorized as being so extraordinary, while I find myself thinking, But it isn't, it's so fucking ordinary.

The first few years after I'd had the mastectomy and Sarah and I were together were awful. They were awful and they were wonderful. I mean, we were – and still are – madly in love with each other. We loved being with each other. We loved every aspect of ourselves. At the same time we were absolutely poverty stricken. The first job I got I was sacked from because I was transsexual. The second job I got they tried to blackmail me 'cos I was transsexual. And I remember thinking, This is it, we're never going to have a life we can live just as ourselves – we're always going to be hiding.

We were constantly torn between trying to keep it a secret and wanting to be open. And we were drastically broke, I mean, broke, broke, broke. I can remember us having a huge row over half a tin of tomatoes, 'cos I said one day, 'Where's the other half of the tin of tomatoes?' And the whole tin had been used, a 17p tin of tomatoes had been used in the meal. The whole tin had been used, and I said, 'Why do you need the whole tin?' That was how broke we were. And yet at the same time there was immense pressure to almost be more middle class than anybody else, to go to work and to do the job better than anybody else, in order to safeguard yourself. We felt we had to appear more normal and more sane than anybody else, there was never any space for us to have our own emotional crises. That was out of the question. Sarah said that if she'd wanted to leave me, where would she go? Because, normally, when women leave their fellas they go to their mother – but she didn't have her mother to go to.

We knew Alex and John – and we had odd friends, but it was very hard. We had some friends who knew, but they were very, very few. We had some transsexual friends, but it was always a case of never meeting at the house. They never came to the house because nobody must ever see. It was like being a Jew in Nazi Germany. I used to say at the time, 'Oh, for God's sake, I wish I was Jewish and then at least I'd know why I was undergoing all this.' And I still say it on occasions when people are being fucking pains in the backside, I say, 'If I were Jewish I would understand it.'

Yet during this time we could pass publicly as a couple with no problems whatsoever. We had this whole bout of me losing jobs. Sarah was nursing, and she was really concerned that if people knew my background it would be the butt of jokes *ad infinitum* –

medicine is a harsh and cruel place. But outwardly we were a nice, respectable couple. There was this total contradiction, and we'd go to London to a drag ball for a moment of sanity.

We stayed in Manchester. We came up to Manchester after I'd finished at university. Sarah had already started her nurse's training and we bought a couple of houses between us. We paid cash for them. Well, we got credit cards out to buy them. They were the kind of houses with no toilets inside, and we renovated them, which took us three years. Then we bought a big house between us, which took another ten years to renovate. We bought it for twenty grand and we sold it for one hundred and twenty. We worked hard.

In 1985, in my second job, I worked for a large charity – which I won't name, much as I want to sometimes. I was head of the finance unit, and there was a scam going on amongst the management group. One day I sat down and realized (a) we were going to go to the wall, we were going to go bust, and (b) they'd set me up, I was going to be the one who ended up with a jail sentence. So I tried very nicely to go round to all the right people and explain that this was going to happen, but nobody would take me seriously. Then the management team had me in and said that if I said anything to anybody I'd find myself all over the *News of the World*. And I just thought, Argh, fuck it, they can say anything to the *News of the World*, I'm not going to go to nick for nobody's sake. And I walked out of the job, and they went bust almost to the day I said they would – 'cos I was good, I was good at my job. Several of them got charged with offences.

This was the second job I'd lost, and my brother had just left the Merchant Navy, and he wanted to set up an engineering company. I went in to do his bookkeeping and things like that. At the same time I started a part-time law degree in the evenings. We had a garage workshop and a bit of boiler engineering on the side. I used to supervise the guys who were working the garage side, and one night in the pub my brother told them that I'd had a sex change, so they just came in one day, packed their tools and went. And that was my savings gone down the drain. But I still see my brother. At the time I can remember Alex saying, 'That's it!' But I said, 'The reality is, this is my family. He may have been a total fucking arsehole, but every time I go to family dos, do we have him walking out or me walking out? You know, I just can't deal with that.' So I went and saw him, sat him down and said to him, 'Do you know what you've just cost me in financial terms, in social terms?'

I started the part-time law degree in September 1985. The garage went the following

February, '86. So I started doing painting and decorating for people, just to make a living, while I carried on with the law degree. In the summer I got a job running a language school here in Manchester, and I did that every summer and Easter vacation for the next five years. I used to enjoy that. I had a colleague who's remained my best friend ever since. And we ran these language schools for a company. Then in the winter I bought another house over the road from where we were renovating. One of the blokes who had worked with me in the summer school and his partner were looking for somewhere to live, so they moved into one of the rooms, and we renovated that. We did all sorts of things, building work, y'know, landscape gardening, painting and decorating, central-heating repairs. We did that right through to 1991–2 and made a reasonable living. We weren't rich, but we made enough money to carry on with the house, and there was always work if we wanted it. We were making enough to be able to say no sometimes.

And I carried on with the law degree. In about 1990 I started the part-time Ph.D. We closed the business down gradually, 'cos we had quite a few lads working for us by the end. They were all rogues, but they all knew my background, they all knew my history and none of them gossiped about it. It wasn't an issue; they were out of the Irish music scene, I was just accepted and that was really nice.

So I got my degree and I really wanted to do a Ph.D. I'd made the decision that I didn't want to be a solicitor. I'd debated the Bar, but it would have meant travelling back and forth to London. So I thought, No, I'm going to be an academic, that's it. I think I'm good enough to do this. I want to do this. So I persuaded them that I wanted to do the Ph.D. and I would pay my own way, 'cos I knew I could just make enough money, and I'd already done the degree part-time. I'd renovated one house, renovated another, brought a team of blokes in. So I thought, I can do this. I applied to do something on crowd control in football and didn't get that. Then I said, 'Well, OK, I'll do transsexuals and the law, which is what I do know about.' And we were sat there, and they said, 'Well, we're a bit concerned about this.' And I said, 'Why?' And they said, 'About your proposal, well, we don't see how you're going to do the research. Nobody can get hold of these people.' And I said, 'Well, I don't think that's really a problem.' And they said, 'Well, hmm, how do you think you're going to do it?' And I said, 'I have lots of contacts.' 'Oh, how come?' And I said, 'Well, because I am one.' And they hadn't had a clue. Their mouths dropped open. But that meant that my supervisor, Steve, after that he just said, 'Yeah, we're gonna do this. You want to do this, you want to be an academic and I'm going to get you through that.'

I'd changed my name by deed poll way back in 1975 when I first transitioned. Then, over the years, I'd gradually changed all my documents. Because I'd had this horrendous experience at Sussex of being out, I'd decided that from then on I was just going to attend part-time classes and mind my own business. As a lawyer I can tell you now that the precise legality of passing is difficult to ascertain. In England you can call yourself anything you want to and it's legal, but you also have aliases, you're 'also known as'. So technically I was Stephen Whittle, also known as. And for things like applications, where gender is requested, I'd just lie, and tick the box marked 'M'. But certainly the basis upon which I lost my first job was that I hadn't been truthful. And I'd contacted the Equal Opportunities Commission and said, 'Have I got any case here? Can I just be dismissed like that?' And they said, 'Well, you know, transsexuals are not protected full stop.' That was another reason for taking the law degree – it was a real incentive, because I was sick of the fact that nobody really knew.

So, I became the first academic legal specialist in transgender issues who is himself a transgender individual. I can see guys coming through in the States now who are similar, and it's really nice to see the next generation coming up and doing it. I've got a friend who works for the National Lesbian Legal Center in the States and he transitioned while working there, so he's their 'other attorney who's a bloke' now. But that wasn't even feasible at the time I did it. It was also a very good reason for me not becoming a solicitor, because I knew I was flannelling it, and I never wanted to be put in a position again where I could work my socks off, do it really well and then get dumped.

During these years we (Sarah and I, along with our friends Alex and John) became family, in part through moving to the last house before this one and working together. And it was fairly clear that we were together for good now and that wasn't going to change. Before we moved here we'd had Eleanor, and we decided we wanted to move because we were right on the border of Moss Side there. It was great for adults, but Sarah said that the first time she went to the playgroup she found herself filling in other people's benefit forms, and she said, 'I just want somebody to look after *me*.' So, when we said we were selling up and moving here everybody immediately asked, 'Oh, and where are Alex and John going?' And we said, 'Well, they're moving with us. This is family.' I don't want to live entirely by ourselves. Believe it or not, we like the fact that we live with other people. This is very much our lives, my politics, everything. My whole nature of being – on the left, queer – relates to the roots of how we live.

We actually ummed and ahed about parenting for a very long time. I don't want to speak out of turn, I don't want to speak for Sarah. But I think my feeling from her was that this whole thing was just too big to deal with, without having that extra dimension as well. She desperately wanted to be a parent – or to have a go at being a parent – this thing was a huge obstacle. And certainly, in the '80s, a couple of times we went to see the doctor, and all we got was, 'Well, it's not possible, not feasible, we won't get anybody to see you.' And partly because they said that, we were able to just leave it. Of course, it was a possibility, but in terms of the provision of AI (Artificial Insemination) in this country, it was very much more difficult. You had the choice of either fighting your way through the clinic system or finding a friend. Well, we weren't in the gay and lesbian community, so finding a friend of that kind was difficult. We talked to my brother, who at one stage offered to be a donor, because he wasn't going to have children. But we all of us took counselling about that. And we had our counselling sessions, and we all met back and said, 'No. Too dicey.' As he said, y'know, the idea of having a family do, and sitting and watching me speak in a certain way to a child which was his biological child could be a disaster. We had a couple of other people make offers, but one backed out at the last minute. Then we tried with one and it just didn't work.

So, all the time there was, 'Oh my God, there's this huge issue there.' Eventually, in 1989, as I was coming up to the end of my law degree, and Sarah was finishing her degree, we said, Well, either she needed to go and get a career or we should think about children seriously. So we sat down and thought about what was entailed. We could try the National Health Service system – but we knew we'd get rejected. We could try the private healthcare system – and we knew that would be uphill. Or, we could have a look and see what other alternatives there were. We contacted a lesbian group in Manchester, and they were really unhappy about talking to a couple that involved a transsexual man. We tried the National Health Service, and our doctor couldn't even get a reply from the hospital, despite writing to them frequently. And we tried various private routes. Then we went to BPAS clinic in Liverpool – the pregnancy and advice service – and we just started treatment with them, we'd gone through the process. Then the 'virgin birth' scandal broke out, and the BPAS closed all their fertility clinics in response to the scandal of this woman having a baby when she had never had sex with a man. We then moved to another clinic, where a creepy guy kept referring to 'my babies' and 'my ladies', and didn't like me to be in the room when he was doing the insemination. Finally, after a whole lot more fighting through the system, we got a private clinic in Manchester to accept us. After the first treatment, Sarah conceived, and eventually Eleanor was born, then a couple more treatments led to Gabriel. We did discuss a lot whether or not to try for a third baby, but as it happens we did give it a go – and then we ended up with twins, Lizzie and Pippa – which was terrifying – I mean, was there enough of me to go around that many people? Well, there isn't, sometimes I feel very thinly spread, but somehow it all works, and being a dad has given my life a whole new perspective, which is pretty exciting as well as being totally knackering.

The best way I can answer the inevitable question, Did you feel like a father?, is to say, there was a group of people who we'd practised our birthing techniques with. And there was a reunion at which we all had our babies lined up on the sofa for a photograph, and I can remember looking at them and thinking, 'Well, I don't know how these people can put up with the fact that our child is just so much more beautiful than theirs. Look at them, they're ugly, they're hideous, they're wrinkly and she is absolutely out of this world. And we were talking in the car home and Sarah had thought exactly the same thing. Of course the other parents were also thinking exactly the same thing about their children. And I look at that photograph now, of all these eight babies, and Eleanor's a bit jaundiced, all wrinkly – she looks like a baby. But when she was born I had this overwhelming sensation, and still, when I see my kids in with a group of other kids, they're always the most beautiful.

I've had to cut off from the kids in order to go away and work on occasions. But I found that having the children was a real bonus for me, in terms of work, because it's given me a real incentive to go to work: maintaining a moral and social obligation to my children, to provide for them. And it also gives me a real reason for coming home: I want to come home and see my children. So, I've dealt with work by actually framing it within the concept of my responsibility as their father – and as their father I also want to come back. I do find the social pressures on being what a father's meant to be like quite hard – the fact that you're meant not to touch your children in the same way that women touch them.

I've also been absolutely knackered. I've nearly always been the person that gets up in the middle of the night, simply because I wake up in the middle of the night anyway. Obviously Sarah did the breastfeeding, but once that finished I was the one who got up, I'm always alert. And I loved those moments in the middle of the night, absolutely loved those moments when there's just them and me, and there's a real sense now of having the closeness of a relationship that you just never get without that contact. There've been times when I've been at work and people have said, 'Oh well, y'know, it's Sarah's job to do that.' And I've said, 'Pardon! Why would I want Sarah to do that?' 'Oh well, then you wouldn't be so tired.' 'No thank you, I'll put up with being tired, this is, like, so special.'

As a father you're also not meant to participate in the decision-making process in the same way. People always have been very willing when you do participate, whether it's with school or the doctor or whatever else, but it's those touchy-feely bits as well. Gabriel loves to stand and have his back stroked by me. He'll lift up his shirt and say, 'Scratch my back, Dad.' My mother will say, 'Leave him alone.' And I'm going, 'Hold on a minute, he's four, he's five, does it matter?' Eleanor is now at the point – she's seven – where she's saying, 'Oh, don't give me a kiss as we're going into school.' Well, thank God I did kiss her on all those other occasions.

I've never felt more affinity with my boy than I have with the girls. I have a completely different relationship with all of them, that's what's really noticeable, and it changes depending on who they are at each stage. Gabriel was awful, at times, for the first three years, so Sarah and I found it really difficult anyway, 'cos there were moments when we were out of our minds with him. He had really bad colic as a baby, he never slept, so we were struggling. But in a sense this was very good, because it made us work hard at making sure we were connected with him. And suddenly he came through it at three and a half, and he's just the most delightful child I could ever imagine at all.

Eleanor I've just always been in love with from the word go. As for Lizzie and Pippa, Lizzie's a delightful little girl, and somehow you can't imagine that you're going to be allowed to keep her, 'cos she's so special and unique. That doesn't make the rest any the less special and unique, but she's so different you can't imagine. But Pippa, she appears a much harder child to get to know – she's much quieter, minds her own business, much more independent. In fact, Lizzie would only be breastfed when she was small, but Pippa would take a bottle. And Lizzie was quite sickly and therefore needed to be breastfed. We tried all sorts of things and we got no sleep, and eventually I moved down into my study and Pippa came into a cot with me, and I used to feed her from a bottle in the middle of the night. This probably went on only for about six months, but I had her entirely to myself. But it was significant, and that was a really nice thing. I often thought that particular process gave me a chance to have the child I couldn't ever have – to have a real physical bond with Pippa, which was the thing that I'd lost. In many ways I felt like I'd been given it back. It was an extra because I'd worked hard – it was a reward to be given Pippa to deal with.

Eleanor knows I'm trans. Gabriel does as well – although I don't know if he susses it completely yet. But Eleanor's got quite a complex understanding of it. We decided we would tell them from the off. This has been a crucially important part of our life. Before we had Eleanor, Sarah and I went to counselling together. Initially this was to talk about what would happen if we didn't have a child, how were we going to maintain the dynamic in a relationship that we really wanted? But in the process of that we also talked about all the issues, like dealing with telling other people about me, to what extent we were going to be out, and the fact that Sarah had felt for a very long time that as soon as people knew about me it refocused their relationship with us in all sorts of different ways. She hated that we were seen as being different, but at the same time she was really pleased that we *were* different.

One of the things that we discussed – and it was almost my precursor before having children – was that if we were going to have children, we had to be out. Because, in my experience, other guys in my situation whose partners had children who were not biologically theirs – and there weren't many – none of them had had their relationships last. This huge secret had been used, ultimately, in the break-up of the relationship, and it had meant that they'd lost the children for periods of time. And there was no way I was going to have that happen to me. I was not going to get involved in having kids in a situation where I could be blackmailed. The second thing we felt really crucially was that if I couldn't stand up and be myself, how on earth could I tell my children to be themselves? And if we couldn't be proud of what I'd done, how on earth could they ever be proud of what I'd done? And I wanted them to be proud of who I was. I felt like I'd done a lot. They can think I'm as bats as buggery – and they will do for some considerable period of time – but I wanted them to understand that they were children we had chosen to have and how much they meant to us.

They'll never quite understand that completely – obviously. But I wanted them to realize that when the day comes that they shout, 'You're not my bloody dad!', and I say back, 'I am your bloody father 'cos there's no other bugger around doing it,' they'll know exactly what I mean, and that I wasn't hurt that they'd said that – but this is the reality, this is who you've got! And maybe we could have a good shouting match, the way fourteen-year-olds do with their parents, without it having to be ultimately hurtful.

I couldn't have done it without Sarah's willingness to examine all of these issues and feelings, it was really crucial, and I don't think for a minute that she found all of these things easy, because I was making more demands on her. But she was willing to give it a go. At the time when Sarah was pregnant with Eleanor things were not easy. Sarah's mother was, 'Ooh, I don't know about this . . .', and they were just beginning to come back together. But once Eleanor was born their relationship was well on the way; and when Gabriel was born, that was it. The fact that we were having a second child affirmed to Sarah's parents that we were continuing and that their attempts to break us up were not going to succeed.

Having the kids was the moment when what we were doing was sorting out where our real lives were situated. And our real lives were situated here, but in order to be fully real they had to include everything, every single aspect, and that included me, and who I was, and how I was, and who I was gonna be.

The way we've told the kids about me is gradually. We're at the point now with the twins of explaining to them about the day they were born. So what we've done is tell them this story, which is, 'This was the day you were born, this is what it was like. Oh look, there's a lot of hair, pull you out, oh it's a girl.' But then we've taken that story back, stage by stage: 'And I went into the clinic to get pregnant because we had to have some sperm, and Dad couldn't make sperm because when Dad was born he looked like a little girl, and everybody thought he was a little girl, but, as you know, he's not.' When the twins were about three months old, we were both feeding them at the living-room table, and Eleanor turned round and said, 'Mum, Dad, how do you know Lizzie and Pippa are girls?' And Sarah and I just looked at each other and we went, 'Mm', and I answered, 'Well, we don't actually know whether they are girls. What we do, just like every other family does, we make an approximate guess. We know that most people born with fannies will grow up to be girls and most people born with willies will grow up to be boys. So we start off somewhere.' Then she said, 'Well, what happens if we've got it wrong?' I said, 'Well, when they're big enough and old enough they'll tell us, just like I told my mum and dad, and then we'll get it sorted out.' And she goes, 'Right.' She knows all about our involvement with Press for Change and transsexual people – and it's so *passé* to her, it's not even an issue. Something happened once at Brownies and I said, 'Oh well, of course, when I was a

Brownie . . .' And she was saying, 'And did you have to wear a Brownie uniform?' 'Yes.' 'But didn't your mum say you looked daft in it?' 'Well, she didn't say I looked daft in it because I didn't look daft in it at that point.'

People often can't imagine this, but I have so little memory of being pre-Stephen; to this date it only ever comes back in nightmares or, as we've done here, we've sat down, talked and got slight flickers of it back. But the actual physical memory is a flicker at most, a sort of strange sensation through my arm or through my body a little bit. I've got certain, momentary images and I've got voices in my head. I've got voices more than anything. Words. It's not even voices, it's words. I can pin together the words to describe what happened, but I don't physically remember it and I don't see it. But I do remember all of that about being Stephen. I have physical memories of being myself. I can describe the first time of, say, going to bed with Sarah, and it's a really strong physical memory. But I can't adequately describe the first time I went to bed with anybody else because I have no memory of it. So, it's almost as if – and it was very early on that I started to do it – I learnt not to memorize. I don't know whether this is learning, but I just stopped remembering. I stopped remembering completely. As a small child I stopped remembering because it was all too horrible. And what's happened for me – or what I feel has happened – is that when I reached forty I thought, Well, I'm about twenty-one now. Then I thought, 'Argh! I'm grown up!', and there was a real sense of feeling that I'd done the time, I'd toed the line and done everything I was meant to do, and I'd been a good boy. Now I can break the rules a bit if I want to because I'm a grown-up. I can choose to eat what I want to eat, I can wear what I want to wear, I can do what I want to do. And it was a real sense of growing up. There were all sorts of things that happened, like my mother stopped sitting on my shoulder every time I was having sex. I had a real life. What I'd had before was a life which was in dribs and drabs, little bits of the picture, the stringing-together of words, and that's very hard to explain to people.

I can remember the 'Peter' stories in great detail – those are the only things I remember. Those are much more real to me. As I said, the only time any of my teenage years or childhood comes back to me now is occasionally in nightmares. I'll have nightmares in which, for example, I'm at Girl Guide camp and I've got a Scout uniform on. Or I'll be on the school platform for something and I'll realize I've got a beard. And I'm trying to piece it all together, y'know, because in these nightmares it's almost like nobody else notices that I'm different but I know I'm really different. In many ways this is exactly a repeat of what did happen. But it's this whole sensation, it's not just that I'm mentally different, I'm physically different and they can't see it at all.

I think what having the kids has done for me is to provide a stage in being a man that most people in my community don't get a chance to experience. It's provided me with an opportunity to experience another aspect of being a man that I never expected to have. One of the things I'd always felt before was that I couldn't quite grow up and I only ever had to look after me *per se*. And it's quite interesting, because looking after the kids has made me much more daring than just looking after me ever did. I mean, I've been much more out – and enjoyed being out. I took Eleanor and Gabriel to Pride (the Gay Pride carnival) a couple of years ago and was able to say to them, 'This is our community. This is where we belong.' I wouldn't ever have taken my mother or my sister or brother or anybody from work, but I took my kids and wanted to introduce them to where I belonged. And at the same time I wanted my community to welcome them as part of it. Sometimes I find myself thinking, Oh my God, what am I doing to my kids? But then I'm also really pleased that I'm doing it, that I want them to have a much queerer upbringing than I ever had. All this means is that I want them to be able to realize the extent to which there are choices. I realize that when you're responsible for kids you don't have to put your desires on them, you can just desire for them what they want.

One of the things my friend Del said to me was, 'Oh, I just love you, Stephen. You're just so queer for somebody who's so straight.' And he wasn't talking about what I did in bed with anybody, he was talking about the fact that I am the archetypal straight person in one sense. I live a straight life. And yet at the same time it's all done in such a queer way.

Talking about the nature of patriarchy, or what a patriarch is, I try to think about it in terms of what it is one tries to be in life. First of all, I don't know whether it's a masculine thing to do, but the majority of the time I do think I know best. And I think I know best because I think I'm the most reasonable and the most rational. Both within the family, and in its relationship with the outer world, and in my relationship with the outer world as well. I fundamentally believe – and this is absolute categorical madness – that I know best, that I'm the most reasonable and rational and thoughtful person I know. The only person who approaches me as being anything like as rational is Sarah. I have friends who are also sometimes reasonable and rational, but they're not actively involved in my life in that way, and they're not having to make those decisions. Often it's I who provide the voice of the reasonable rationalist within their lives. That, I think, is the reality. I work harder than most of the people I know, I'm the most prepared to listen, and I'm the most prepared to admit when I'm wrong. Well, if that's what being a patriarch is, then that's exactly, precisely, what I think a person in a position of power should be.

It's very difficult to explain, because it's not about having power for the sake of power, or being in charge, or taking things from other people, or having my life at the expense of other people; it's about ensuring that everybody gets a fair whack at everything, about taking your responsibilities seriously. Sarah's always saying to me, 'You know, the problem with you, Stephen, is you always want to make it right for everybody and sometimes you just can't.' Particularly like when her mum died, she said, 'Stephen, you just can't make this any better.' And yes, that's what I want to do. I want to make it better for everybody.

I do think masculinity is facing a massive crisis. What it is to be a man has in itself become so inherently devalued — probably rightly so, through feminist discussion, theory and argument — but, at the same time, the reality is that there's no alternative being provided. We talk about the New Man, the 'nice' New Man, and then women say, 'But I don't want the "nice" New Man.' Or lots of women say they don't. If you push them towards a 'nice' New Man, on the whole they go 'Waargh!' I'm often there being a semi-dating agency for other F-to-Ms. And if there are women who say, 'I can't stand this, I'm straight, but I can't stand the straight men I know,' I say 'OK, I'll introduce you to some really nice straight men.' And it works.

But there's no new model of masculinity. And I think one of the things I've learnt through being a transsexual man, is that transsexual men, we've worked very hard to provide an alternative model of masculinity, because we've inculcated those sort of values, an awful lot of us have come out of the lesbian/feminist community; if nothing else, we sat and we discussed this *ad infinitum*: what were better values.

I was thinking about suddenly becoming a man with Sarah, and the truth is, my masculinity was always there, and it was the bone of contention with everybody else. The masculinity's always, always been there. My mother's argued about it, people at school argued about it, the doctors argued about it, somehow it wasn't meant to be there, but it was always there. What Sarah did was enable me to step over the line into becoming a man with that masculinity. And I've often thought about that since: Well, should I actually have stood out to be a woman who was masculine? But of course that was never me. I could have done that quite easily — but it would never have been me.

There were a couple of other guys I know who have long-term partnerships with women, and who spend quite a lot of time away working, and we had this joke going that, basically, you pay for the tickets, you pay for the hotel, you hire the tux, just in order to have sex for the night . . . and it would be much cheaper to go to a prostitute. Now, one of the straight men that we had this joke with, the fact that I'm trans is not an issue to him, but a lot of the other guys will have the joke until I walk into the room, and then they get very uncomfortable. They cannot deal with my sexuality. You can see them thinking, Well, what does he do? How does he do it?, whereas all my gay male friends accept the fact completely that I have the genitals I have. They're not in the slightest bit fussed. They view me as having a dick, but a small dick. They view me as having other bits – but just as having 'other bits'. They say, 'You're so lucky having so many bits, I wish I did.' I've never, ever met any gay man from the most masculine, butch, leather guy, who is totally penis-orientated, to the campest of camp, who has ever, ever, not regarded me as simply one of the men.

For myself, I find it's a fearful future. I can't deal at all, mentally, with the notion that one day I might end up old and gaga, or physically unable to look after myself, in a nursing home, no matter what anybody else says. I was talking to a doctor the other day, and he said, 'You've got to remember, when you're old everybody's desexualized.' Yes, they may be, but that doesn't mean you're less of a sexual person. It's simple things like going to the toilet – I don't want nurses wiping my bum. I don't want them to see what I've got. I don't mind people I sleep with seeing what I've got, but I don't want people I'm not sleeping with seeing. I don't want them talking behind my back.

I see my elderly friends now reaching their deaths. I've seen them labelled as 'female' on their death certificates. I've seen their families bury them as women, and I've seen doctors put them in women's wards. I think I'd go mad. Absolutely stark-fucking-raving bonkers. Completely. I had to have a minor operation on a pile, and I went to see the doctor first, and I said, 'Right, let's get this straight, when I go to that operating theatre, this is going to be done under local, and there will not be one smirk on anybody's face.' And he said, 'Oh no, no-no.' And I said, 'Absolutely, get it straight, I don't want to see a twinkle in anybody's eyes. I'm not interested. I'm not going to have it done unless that is categorically understood, down the line. I don't care what they say behind my back, but I don't see it and I don't hear it.' And they all kept completely straight faces and were very nice.

I am debating having cosmetic surgery to create a phallus, which would be non-functioning. And the whole idea of this surgery is that it would remove nothing. Everything would be kept completely intact, but I'd have it on the surface, if somebody just looked at me, physically. I'm not sure whether I'm going to do it or not. I found a surgeon – he's a nice bloke, he does a good job. He does stuff for guys who've lost their penises in fires, or accidents, but it's not that brilliant. You'd always look like you had a dick which had had an operation on it.

It's a bit like growing the beard in some senses; well, growing the beard I did for me, but in some ways I was also making a statement to the wider world. And with this, I might be able to go in and use the shower or just feel more relaxed in certain circumstances. This is partly what I want – that extra little bit. This time, Sarah's said, 'This is absolutely your choice, Stephen. This is not a decision I am going to participate in.' As far as she's concerned, the biggest issue for her is that everything else is left completely intact, that's what bothers her: that we can have the sex life we have, and a good one.

I find the idea of having something that's like a penis – because that's all it is – and having intimate sexual intercourse with Sarah, the most appealing idea. Even, maybe, without much sensation. But the idea of being able to do that is what I've always wanted; it's a thing I've always missed. Yet at the same time it doesn't matter. It really doesn't matter. It's never mattered. But it's still something that I really miss. It's like being told you can never eat chips again. And obviously I don't know what it's like to have a large penis, but what I do know is what I have and how it feels. It feels like a penis, it feels like a dick. Maybe it's small but it's pretty good.

As for acceptance in the wider world, last year when I did my lecture where I tell the students about myself, somebody sniggered. And by God, it was twenty minutes before I let them out of that room, 'cos I let rip. There are ways and ways of behaving in public – I don't snigger about their issues and they don't snigger about mine. My tolerance levels for that have completely gone. I'm not intolerant of anybody, y'know. I might be intolerant of members of the BNP (the British National Party, a fascist group), but I have to be pushed fucking far.

As for the legal status of transgender people, I feel really torn. Part of me is incredibly optimistic, because I can't imagine that we can carry on like we did. If we can't do it with this government we're never going to do it. My feelings are, with this government (the Labour administration of Tony Blair), is that if they get in on a second term we've got a good chance of resolving most of the problems. We won't resolve everything, but we'll get some moves. And I feel very optimistic about that; I do feel that their hearts are in the right places. But if that doesn't happen, it's not going to happen in my lifetime. If I don't see something in two years I won't see anything.

Of course, one of the biggest things we have found ourselves discovering at governmental levels is how can we do this without it being seen? What can we do? How can we avoid a backlash? And we have done quite a lot of things in relation to driving licences and the employment issues, by keeping it so low. Simple things, like they haven't sent out the press releases they normally would. We can disseminate the news through our community – if they try and do it, it gets disseminated to the wrong people. I don't care in one sense, whether anything ever is done, but I do really care that if it's not done, it's because there's an incredible amount of bigotry existing amongst people.

My suspicion about gender, as somebody who has read the scientific material in the area, and as a lawyer, though, is that, yes, it probably is biologically determined. I don't think it matters, but I think there's a significant body of evidence now coming out from animal experiments, brain studies, and so on, that actually clearly places gender identity – not gender role – in a way that is biologically determined. This is problematic, because it obviously has cultural and social implications. And the research that has been done so far has been done on Western populations or animal populations. So, how do you stretch the point? But one of the things that provides a basis for understanding is that when you look at trans representations in different cultural environments, trans still exists but it will be differently culturally represented. So, within whatever framework it's in, there will be a different understanding, but the individuals still exist. If you put a modern European context on to their lives, you'd say, 'Oh yes, these people are transsexual.' By reading their life stories you would see it but, of course, it's framed in a completely different way. Which is why I deduce from the research that's come out that there is probably a biological determinant to gender, but that it's culturally potentiated in a myriad of different ways.

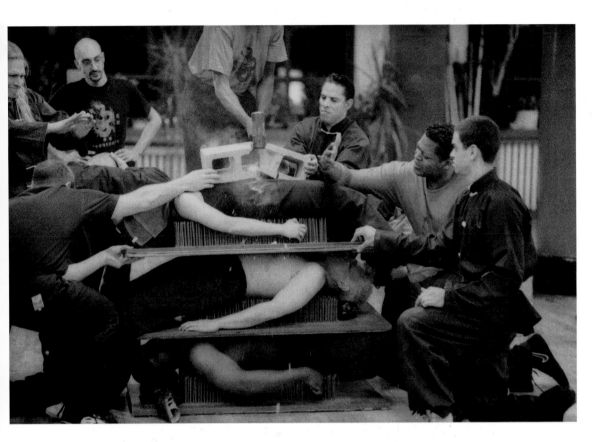

Conclusion

To my mind, Stephen Whittle exhibits one of the characteristics which, if not by any means confined to men, has often been used to define us: bravery. He has lived his life with courage, and in speaking openly and honestly about it, he does battle bravely with the small-minded and fearful bigotry that always lies in wait to attack – and where possible destroy – any significant measure of human difference, whether that of race, or creed, or sexual orientation, or gender.

It is not often in adult life that we're given the opportunity to have our preconceptions altered; for the convictions of another to impact on us and become canonical. In my conversations with Stephen I came to believe that he was what he said he was – a man; and that, further, there must be others like him, people who while possessing the sexual characteristics of one gender nonetheless know themselves to be the other. I'm not saying that I gave no credence to the concept of gender dysphoria before meeting Stephen, but along with all sorts of theories used to explain modes of being that diverge from the accepted social norms, I looked upon it at best as being an approximation – a catch-all to explain a bundle of probably pathological conditions – and at worst as being a mystification.

Stephen is himself explicit about his own gender status; while he identifies himself as being a 'man', he does not claim to be one. He understands that his is a third way. But who's to say how many ways there may be? Stephen sees masculinity as a biologically determined state that is subsequently potentiated by social factors, then reinforced by cultural ones. In his own case he has had to supply his own potentiators, in the form of male hormones, male clothes and other masculine signifiers. But most defining for him was the acceptance of who he was that was supplied by the unconditional love of his partner.

Stephen is emphatic about quite how much it means to him to be able to pass as a man in social situations. He goes so far as to imply that the main reason he might want a pseudo-penis would be in order to have showers, or get changed, in male-only contexts. In other words – to pass more fully. He does not need these attributes either for himself, or for those closer to him than showering men, because their view of him, and his own, already correspond.

Surely this analysis of masculinity, and what it is to be a man, holds true for all of us? (I say 'all of us', but my remarks in what follows are mainly directed towards heterosexual men. I don't doubt that homosexual men experience their own crises surrounding gender, but they don't tend to rape women because of a sense of impotent rage.) We are all born with obvious gender signifiers that prompt a response from those who behold us; and as we grow, these accrete to form the person – man or woman – who others believe us to be. In parallel, we develop our own conception of who we want to be – and what kind of person that is. Who we truly are exists in the reciprocal accommodations, and consequent adjustments, that are constantly being visited upon these conceptions: the inner and the outer. Fulfilment – as a man, as a woman, as a writer, as a veterinary surgeon – could be said to exist when these are in harmony with one another. So, the cartoon adulterous man says to the cartoon woman he's just fucked: 'My wife doesn't understand me.' But what he should say is: 'My understanding doesn't wife me.' For clearly, there's no accord between his conception of himself as a man – and how others see him.

In a world in which to be a man is no longer a matter of subduing enemies by force, and thereby protecting women and children, what physical aspects of masculinity can be said to be important? What honour is there within physical masculinity if it isn't important for breadwinning? After all, the *sine qua non* of an occupation that unmans in our era is that it be wholly manual. I think Stephen Whittle's experience has valuable things to tell us about what's wrong with the rust bowl – if not what kind of industry should replace it.

The problem for most of us who call ourselves 'men' is that far from having to decide whether or not we want a penis, or muscles, or a beard – it's those things that appear most given to us, and hence most defining of us. So, in a world that has no obvious use for our muscles, we seek to identify ourselves with those men for whom they're still functionally required: professional athletes, and the action heroes in movies. We scream impotent obscenities on the football stands, and gawp in the multiplex, awed by these spectacles of masculine physical utility. We vicariously bomb the Balkans. By the same token, we over-sexualize the world and our place in it, because all we have to guarantee that we will be regarded as men is our penetrating penises. Surely – we unreason – if we can be seen to screw Ceres, then she'll know what men we are? And in a world without a viable definition of male honour, of how it is to behave as a man should in respect of women, the importance of quantifiers – sizes, numbers – will swell up to alarming proportions. They may well become all that matters.

For most people who call themselves 'men' it's all too easy nowadays to merely 'pass' as one. When the deception is uncovered, the pseudo-man can always retreat to being one of the boys, with the assurance that they're the people who're least likely to launch a full enquiry.

I began this text with a short memoir of my own father, because he was the man in whose proximity I came into the world and into myself – he was my paradigm of masculinity. When he died I was younger than he was when I was born. It was odd to realize that I would come to know him more intimately through the experience of being the age he was when I first knew him than I ever did while he was alive. For we come to know our same-gender parents through the mannerisms we share with them, the reflex actions that seal our fate as their biological inheritors. If we are men, we become close to our fathers through our coughs, our laughs and the way we hold our cigarettes. To paraphrase Wilde (who my father would have called 'dear old Oscar', as if they'd recently shared some oysters in the Café Royale together), every man comes to resemble his father – that is his tragedy.

And in this genetic acquaintance, I sense, more than ever, the extent to which our shared masculinity is merely a set of basic, physical attributes, with no more significance than five toes, or earlobes. I do not wish to speak ill of the dead, but on balance I'd rather not be my father's son – and would much prefer to be Stephen Whittle's.

vi Posters on wall, New York

15 A. Piddington, Gramercy Park, New York

16 Six weeks, London

17 Eleven months, London

18/19 Boules-playing, Provence

20 School stop, Thailand

21 Rubber mask and plastic gun, Luxembourg

22/23 Disused fairground, the former Soviet Union

24 East End boys, London

25 Boy with gun, the former East Germany

26 Punk, west London

 **32/33** Checking out the car, New York

 **27** Reflection, New York

 **34** Hanging out, Provence

 **28/29** Rollerskating, Paris

 **35** National Front march, London

30 Finals day, Oxford

 **31** Russian sailors, Ireland

 **36** Torture protest, New York

 **37** Nightclub, London

 **38/39** Chelsea cruise, London

 **46** S. Whittle with Lizzie, Stockport

 **40** Marlboro Man, Los Angeles

 **97** Stone circle, Cornwall

 **41** Cowboy-clothes shop, Nashville

 **98** Couple in a lift, London

 **42/43** Drinking bar, London

 **99** Street show, Paris

 **44/45** Luxembourg Gardens, Paris

 **100** Westminster, London

 **101** Marvellous Phil, London

 **102** F. Barrat, boxer, London

 **103** Boxing club, London

 **104** Graffiti, Rome

 **105** F. Bruno after world-title fight, London

 **106** Vice detectives, Florence

 **107** Martial arts, New York

 **108** Photographer, the former Soviet Union

 **109** Bed of nails, New York

 **110/111** Evangelist, London

 **112/113** Swan, K. Kesey magic bus, Stonehenge

 **114** Devil's hat, London

 **115** Distillery, Scotland

 **116** Staten Island ferry, New York

 **117** Bar, New Orleans

 **118** Hallowe'en, New York

 **119** Smoking cigar, New York

 **120/121** King's College, Cambridge

 **122** L. Amellio, art dealer, Naples

 **126** Night out, New York

 **127** Bus stop, the former Soviet Union

 **128/129** Chef, Suffolk

 **130** Street-seller, New York

 **131** Lone swimmer, Provence

 **132/133** Camargue horsemen, Provence

 **134** Monk, Thailand

 **135** S. Hawking, scientist, Cambridge

 **136** Mental institution, Lisbon

 **137** D. Hockney, artist, London

 **138/139** Man in suit, Sicily

 **140** Opium joint, Thailand

 **141** Liberty foam hats, New York

 **145** A. Warhol's wig on his dresser, New York

 **142** Walking, the former Soviet Union

 **146** Christ, Bordeaux

 **143** J. Bratby, artist, Hastings

 **147** Skeletons, Royal Academy, London

 **144** Q. Crisp in his room, New York

My sincere thanks to all those who appear in the photographs.